C000245352

A
ZEST
FOR
LIFE

DD
COOK
BOOK

FRESH, TASTY RECIPES THAT WILL PUT A SPRING IN YOUR STRIDE!

This book is packed full of colourful, energising recipes, made with ingredients that taste great and also help you to feel great!

More than just five-a-day; cooking from this book could give you at least seven of your daily vegetables and fruit, plus plenty of wholegrains and healthy protein.

With superfoods galore and meals that keep you full for longer, this collection of clever, nutritious recipes is one that you'll turn to time and again.

And the fresh and tasty recipes will make eating well effortless, as they are easy to prepare and absolutely delicious. Plus, all the ingredients suggested are widely available – no faddy foods here.

There's a gorgeous colour photograph for every recipe. And each recipe gives you nutritional information on calorie and fat content, as well as salt, sugar and fibre. It shows you which recipes are suitable for vegetarians and vegans, and which can be frozen.

There are also helpful cook's tips to ensure success every time. And, as always, each recipe is triple-tested so you know it will work.

Here, you'll find all the recipes you need for a healthy lifestyle today, in one handy, lie-flat cookbook.

RECIPE NOTES

Nutritional information has been calculated by portion or item. Where there are portion variations, e.g. serves 6-8, the analysis given is based on the larger number. Sugar is 'free sugars' (added sugars, including those naturally present in fruit juice and syrups)

Spoon measures are level unless otherwise stated.

Eggs are large unless otherwise stated in the ingeredients.

(V) Suitable for vegetarians, provided a suitable cheese, yogurt or pesto etc. is used.

(V) Suitable for vegans provided the non-dairy options are chosen, and no honey is added.

(F) Suitable for freezing.

SAFETY NOTES

Recipes using nuts or nut products are not suitable for young children or those with a nut allergy.

Certain at-risk groups, such as pregnant women, babies and sick or elderly people should not eat raw or lightly cooked eggs.

BOUNTIFUL BREAKFASTS

TROPICAL MORNING

Serves 4 Preparation 10 minutes

Oranges 2
Carrot 1, peeled and sliced
Grated root ginger 1 tsp
Tropical/exotic fruit mix, frozen or fresh 225g (8oz)
Lime 1, juice from ½, the other ½ cut into 4 wedges

Cut the peel off the oranges then segment them, catching the juice.

Put the fruit and juice in a blender with the carrot, ginger, tropical fruit mix, the lime juice and 150ml (¼ pint) cold water. Whizz until well blended.

Pour into four tumblers and squeeze in extra lime juice to taste.

Tips

Segment the oranges the night before and keep in the fridge to save time in the morning. Alternatively, you can blend the mixture the night before and keep in the fridge overnight; stir before serving.

NOTES

Calories	Fibre	Salt	Sugar	Fat
60	2.9g	0.1g	0.1g	0.4g of which 0.1g is saturated

Scan QR Code
for an ingredients
shopping list

ROAST AUTUMN FRUIT COMPÔTE

Serves 4   Preparation 15 minutes plus cooling   Cooking 1 hour 5 minutes

Plums 6–8, halved and stoned

Ripe pears 2 small, peeled, cored and halved

Cooking apple 250g (9oz), peeled, cored and cut into chunks

Cranberry juice 250ml (9fl oz)

Clear honey 50g (2oz)

Vanilla pod 1, split lengthways and cut in half

Cinnamon stick 1 small, broken in half

Preheat the oven to 180°C/160°fan/Gas 4.

Place the plums cut-side up in a shallow baking dish. Add the pears and apple chunks then pour over the cranberry juice and drizzle with honey. Push the vanilla and cinnamon among the fruit. Cover with foil and bake for 30 minutes.

Remove the foil, turn the fruit over and return to the oven, uncovered, for a further 30 minutes, basting occasionally, until the fruit is tender.

Using a slotted spoon, lift out the fruit and place in a heatproof dish. Discard the vanilla and cinnamon.

Strain the cooking juices into a small saucepan and bring to the boil. Boil for about 5 minutes or until reduced by half. Pour over the fruit and leave to cool completely, then cover and chill until ready to serve. Enjoy on its own or serve with yogurt, or spoon over breakfast cereal or warm pancakes.

Tips

Peaches, nectarines or apricots, halved and stoned, will also work in this recipe. Use orange or apple juice instead of cranberry if you prefer. To serve as a dessert, replace the cranberry juice with fruity white or red wine, or grape juice.

NOTES

Scan QR Code
for an ingredients
shopping list

Calories	Fibre	Salt	Sugar	Fat
133	3.9g	0g	17g	0.3g of which 0g is saturated

HOMEMADE MUESLI

Serves 2   Preparation 20 minutes

Porridge oats 50g (2oz)

Toasted flaked almonds 40g (1½oz), plus extra to sprinkle

Milk 225ml (8fl oz)

Dessert apple 1 small, cored

Clementine or satsuma 1, peeled and segmented

Raspberries 10

Natural yogurt 4 tbsp

Clear honey 1–2 tsp

Divide the oats and almonds equally between two serving bowls. Stir in the milk and leave to stand for 5–10 minutes.

Meanwhile, chop the apple and clementine or satsuma.

Sprinkle the chopped fruit and the raspberries over the oats. Top with yogurt and sprinkle over a few more almonds. Drizzle with honey, to taste.

Tip

This recipe is really versatile: use any combination of nuts and fruit that you have available.

NOTES

Calories	Fibre	Salt	Sugar	Fat
371	3.4g	0.3g	6.1g	16.2g of which 3g is saturated

Scan QR Code
for an ingredients
shopping list

APPLE & PEAR QUINOA PORRIDGE WITH BLUEBERRIES

Serves 2   Preparation 5 minutes   Cooking 25 minutes

Quinoa 75g (3oz), rinsed and drained

Apple juice 500ml (18fl oz)

Ground cinnamon ½–1 tsp

Porridge oats 3 tbsp

Ready-to-eat dried apricots 4, snipped into small pieces

Greek yogurt or coconut yogurt 2 generous tbsp

Ripe pear 1, quartered, cored and diced

Blueberries 2 handfuls (approx. 50g/2oz)

Chopped pistachio nuts 2 tbsp

Clear honey or maple syrup 1–2 tsp (optional)

Put the quinoa in a small pan with the apple juice and cinnamon to taste. Bring to the boil over a high heat. Cover, reduce the heat and simmer gently for 15–20 minutes until tender and the consistency of porridge; most of the apple juice will have been absorbed.

Take off the heat and stir in the oats and dried apricots.

Spoon into bowls and top with yogurt, pear, blueberries and pistachios. Drizzle with honey or maple syrup if you like.

Tips

You can make this the night before and divide it between two bowls. Cool, cover and chill. To serve, reheat in the microwave on High for 2-3 minutes, then add the toppings. Use pumpkin or sunflower seeds instead of pistachios if you like. Instead of pear and blueberries, try the porridge with apple and dates, or raspberries and dried apricots.

NOTES

Calories	Fibre	Salt	Sugar	Fat
549	10.8g	0.2g	23.1g	18.6g of which 4.2g is saturated

TOASTED TORTILLAS WITH BERRY SALSA

Serves 4   Preparation 10 minutes   Cooking 4 minutes

Strawberries 175g (6oz)

Raspberries 50g (2oz)

Blackberries 50g (2oz)

Blueberries 75g (3oz)

Clear honey 2 tbsp

Low fat soft cheese 200g (7oz)

Ground cinnamon ½ tsp

Soft flour tortillas 8 mini

First make the salsa. Wash and pat dry all the berries. Hull the strawberries and mash with a fork. Crush the raspberries and blackberries lightly with a fork and stir into the strawberries along with the whole blueberries and 1 tablespoon honey. Set aside.

Mix the soft cheese with the cinnamon and the remaining honey until well blended. Set aside.

Just before serving, preheat the grill to hot. Cut the tortillas in half and toast in two batches for a few seconds on each side until lightly golden.

To serve, cut the toasted tortillas in half again and serve with the soft cheese and berry salsa.

Tips

Use your favourite combination of fresh berries. For a tropical alternative, mash chopped fresh mango with ripe banana, add a squeeze of lime juice, and mix in pomegranate seeds.

NOTES

Calories	Fibre	Salt	Sugar	Fat
173	4.1g	0.5g	8.7g	3.2g of which 1.4g is saturated

Scan QR Code
for an ingredients
shopping list

BERRY, GRANOLA & BANANA MUFFINS

Makes 12   Preparation 10 minutes plus cooling   Cooking 30 minutes

Wholewheat plain flour 225g (8oz)

Baking powder 2 tsp

Light brown sugar 110g (4oz)

Berry granola 110g (4oz), crushed, plus extra to sprinkle

Egg 1 medium, beaten

Sunflower oil 125ml (4fl oz)

Whole milk 200ml (7fl oz)

Ripe banana 1 large, peeled and mashed

Vanilla extract 1 tsp

Blueberries 150g (5oz)

Preheat the oven to 190°C/170°fan/Gas 5. Line a 12-hole muffin tin with paper cases.

Put the flour and baking powder in a bowl, stir in the sugar and granola, and make a well in the centre. Pour in the egg, oil and milk and mix carefully until you have a thick batter. Stir in the banana, vanilla and blueberries.

Divide the mixture between the paper cases (they will be quite full), sprinkle with a little granola and bake for 25–30 minutes until risen and lightly golden. Transfer to a wire rack to cool slightly. Best served warm.

Tips

Use your favourite granola or muesli in this recipe. Instead of the blueberries, try other berries such as raspberries or blackberries.

NOTES

Calories	Fibre	Salt	Sugar	Fat
254	1.6g	0.3g	10.4g	12.5g of which 2.1g is saturated

MUFFINS WITH MUSHROOMS & SCRAMBLED EGGS

Serves 4   Preparation 10 minutes   Cooking 10 minutes

Olive oil 1 tbsp

Spring onions 4, trimmed and sliced

Mushrooms 400g (14oz) mixture of small flat, closed cup and chestnut, wiped, trimmed and sliced

Chopped parsley 2 tbsp, plus extra to serve (optional)

Eggs 8

Double cream 125ml (4fl oz)

Salt and freshly ground black pepper

Butter 25g (1oz)

Cheddar and black pepper muffins 4, halved and toasted

Heat the oil in a large non-stick frying pan, add the spring onions and cook for a minute or so, stirring. Add the mushrooms and continue cooking over a high heat, stirring frequently, for about 5 minutes or until the onions are cooked and turning golden. Add the parsley for the last minute of cooking, if using.

Meanwhile, beat together the eggs and cream with salt and pepper. Melt the butter in a separate large non-stick pan and, when foaming, add the egg mix. Cook over a gentle heat, stirring, until softly scrambled.

Pop the hot toasted muffins onto warmed plates. Spoon over the mushrooms, top with the scrambled eggs and serve at once with extra chopped parsley to garnish, if using.

Tips

Use any combination of your favourite fresh mushrooms and, if you like onions, add a few more chopped spring onions to cook with the mushrooms. Choose plain English muffins if you prefer.

NOTES

Calories	Fibre	Salt	Sugar	Fat
557	3.1g	1.8g	0g	37.1g of which 17.4g is saturated

Scan QR Code for an ingredients shopping list

PACKED LUNCHES

VIETNAMESE BANH MI

Serves 2–3   Preparation 15 minutes   Cooking 5 minutes

Carrot 1, peeled

Red cabbage approx. 50g (2oz), finely shredded

Radishes 4, trimmed and sliced

White wine vinegar 2 tbsp

Caster sugar 1 tsp

Salt and freshly ground black pepper

Eggs 3

Spring onions 3, trimmed and sliced

Soy sauce 1 tsp

Vegetable oil 1 tbsp

Baguettes 2 or 3 small

Hummus about 4 tbsp

Chopped fresh coriander 2 tbsp

Hot or sweet chilli sauce to serve (optional)

Make strips of carrot using a julienne cutter and put in a bowl with the red cabbage and radishes. Add the vinegar, sugar and ½ teaspoon salt, mix well.

Beat the eggs in a bowl, add the spring onions, plenty of pepper and the soy sauce.

Heat the oil in a frying pan, pour in the egg mixture and cook for a few minutes on each side to make an omelette. Tip out of the pan onto a board. Roll it up then cut into strips.

Split the baguettes and spread hummus over the cut sides. Pile omelette strips onto the bases, top with the pickled vegetables and sprinkle with coriander. Add the tops of the baguettes to make sandwiches. Serve with chilli sauce if using.

Tips

If you don't have a julienne cutter use a peeler for the carrot. Instead of hummus and omelette, try spreading the baguettes with chicken liver pâté and add cooked chicken or turkey along with the pickled vegetables.

NOTES

Calories	Fibre	Salt	Sugar	Fat
482	6.6g	1.9g	1g	20.2g of which 3.3g is saturated

Scan QR Code
for an ingredients
shopping list

FETA, OLIVE & TOMATO MUFFINS

Makes 9 Preparation 15 minutes plus cooling Cooking 30 minutes

Gluten-free plain flour 150g (5oz)

Polenta 100g (3½oz)

Baking powder 2 tsp

Salt and freshly ground black pepper

Eggs 3 medium, beaten

Whole milk 75ml (3fl oz)

Olive oil 75ml (3fl oz)

Feta cheese 100g (3½oz), crumbled

Pimento-stuffed green olives 100g (3½oz), chopped

Sun-blush tomatoes in oil 100g (3½oz), drained well and chopped

Mixed pumpkin and sunflower seeds 40g (1½oz)

Green salad to serve (optional)

Preheat the oven to 190°C/170°fan/Gas 5. Line a muffin tin with nine paper cases.

Put the flour, polenta and baking powder in a bowl. Season lightly and make a well in the centre. Pour in the eggs, milk and oil and mix carefully to form a thick batter. Stir in the cheese, olives and tomatoes.

Divide the mixture between the paper cases (they will be quite full), sprinkle with a few seeds and bake for about 30 minutes, until risen and lightly golden. Transfer to a wire rack to cool. Eat warm or cold with a green salad if you like.

Tips

Use ground almonds instead of polenta for a richer bake. Replace the olive oil with the oil from the tomatoes for extra flavour. If you're following a gluten-free diet check the label of the baking powder to ensure that no wheat starch has been added. If you're not, you could use ordinary plain flour.

NOTES

Calories	Fibre	Salt	Sugar	Fat
327	1.8g	1.5g	0g	22.3g of which 4.7g is saturated

FETA & STRAWBERRY SALAD

Serves 2   Preparation 20 minutes

Olive oil 2 tbsp

Balsamic vinegar 2 tsp

Red onion ½, peeled and sliced into thin rings

Cucumber ½, quartered, deseeded and sliced

Radishes 4, trimmed and finely sliced

Kalamata olives 10, pitted

Strawberries 200g (7oz), hulled and quartered

Freshly ground black pepper

Mint leaves a good handful

Feta cheese 110g (4oz)

Crusty bread to serve (optional)

Whisk the oil and vinegar together in a large serving bowl. Add the onion, cucumber, radishes, olives and strawberries. Season with black pepper. Set aside for 10 minutes.

Tear most of the mint leaves into the salad and mix gently. Break the Feta into large chunks over the top. Garnish with more mint leaves and serve with your favourite crusty bread if liked.

Tips

Peel the cucumber if you prefer. You could use a British, crumbly white cheese, such as Wensley-dale in place of the Feta.

NOTES

Calories	Fibre	Salt	Sugar	Fat
304	5.8g	1.8g	0g	24.3g of which 9.4g is saturated

Scan QR Code for an ingredients shopping list

TERIYAKI SALMON NOODLE SALAD

Serves 2 Preparation 15 minutes plus cooling   Cooking 10 minutes

Soba noodles 100g (3½oz)

Frozen edamame beans 150g (5oz)

Mangetout 75g (3oz), trimmed and thinly sliced

Smoked salmon 100g (3½oz), sliced into thin strips

Sesame seeds 4 tsp, toasted

Black sesame seeds 2 tsp (optional)

Teriyaki marinade 2 tbsp

Sesame oil 2 tsp

Clear honey 2 tsp

Pea shoots 25g (1oz)

Bring a pan of water to the boil, add the noodles, stir, then cook for about 5 minutes until tender. Drain and rinse in cold running water. Drain well and leave to cool completely, then chill until required.

Bring another pan of water to the boil and add the edamame beans, bring back to the boil, cover and cook for 4 minutes. Add the mangetout and cook for a further minute. Drain and rinse in cold running water. Drain well and leave to cool completely, then chill until required.

When ready to assemble, tip the noodles into a large bowl and toss in the vegetables, smoked salmon and sesame seeds. Mix the teriyaki marinade with the oil and honey and pour over the salad. Toss well and serve topped with pea shoots.

Tips

For your packed lunch, pack the noodles, beans, mangetout and salmon in a sealable container with the pea shoots on top. Keep the dressing in a small jar and mix into your salad just before eating. Soba noodles are made from buckwheat and are naturally gluten-free. You can find them in the Asian section of large supermarkets. Use another type of noodle if you prefer. If you are on a gluten-free diet, use gluten-free teriyaki marinade.

NOTES

Calories	Fibre	Salt	Sugar	Fat
507	11.6g	3.5g	7.6g	19g of which 5.6g is saturated

SALMON & ASPARAGUS SALAD WITH GRAINS

Serves 2 Preparation 20 minutes Cooking 10 minutes

Eggs 2
Fine asparagus tips 100g pack, trimmed
Ready-to-eat mixed grains 250g pack
Rocket salad 60g bag
Kiln-roast Scottish salmon flakes 100g pack
Lemon 1 small, juice only
Olive oil 2 tbsp
Dijon mustard ½ tsp or to taste
Salt and freshly ground black pepper

Put the eggs in a pan of boiling water, cover and simmer for 8 minutes, until hard boiled. Peel and quarter each egg.

Meanwhile, blanch the asparagus in boiling water for 2 minutes until just tender. Drain and refresh under cold water.

Mix the grains with the asparagus, rocket and salmon.

Whisk together the lemon juice, oil and mustard and season to taste.

Divide the salad between two plates, add the eggs and serve with the dressing.

Tips

For your packed lunch, pack the grain salad in a lunchbox. Keep the dressing in a small jar and mix into your salad just before eating. Use canned tuna instead of salmon, if you prefer.

NOTES

Calories	Fibre	Salt	Sugar	Fat
547	5.9g	3.2g	0g	30.4g of which 6.6g is saturated

Scan QR Code
for an ingredients
shopping list

PRAWN & COUSCOUS SALAD

Serves 2 Preparation 15 minutes plus cooling

Couscous 110g (4oz)
Sun-dried tomato paste 1 tbsp
Chicken stock 200ml (7fl oz), boiling
Cooked king prawns 150g (5oz)
Tomatoes 2, diced
Cucumber 7cm (3in) piece, diced
Frozen peas 75g (3oz), cooked
Chopped fresh mint 2–3 tbsp
Salt and freshly ground black pepper

Place the couscous in a large bowl. Stir the sun-dried tomato paste into the boiling stock then pour onto the couscous. Stir, cover and leave for 5 minutes.

Fluff up the couscous with a fork and leave to cool.

Stir in all the remaining ingredients, season to taste and serve.

Tip

To make this recipe suitable for vegetarians, use vegetable stock and griddled Halloumi instead of the prawns

NOTES

Calories	Fibre	Salt	Sugar	Fat
325	5.7g	3.2g	0g	3g of which 0.3g is saturated

PRAWN PITTAS

Serves 2   Preparation 3 minutes

Caerphilly cheese 25g (1oz), crumbled

Cooked prawns 150g (5oz)

Spring onions 2, trimmed and sliced

Tomato 1, chopped

Cucumber 5cm (2in) piece, chopped

Salt and freshly ground black pepper

Natural yogurt 2 tbsp

Dill 1 sprig, chopped (optional)

Pitta bread 2, halved

Mix the cheese, prawns, spring onions, tomato and cucumber together. Season to taste.

Mix the yogurt with the dill, if using.

Split the pitta bread open to form pockets. Divide the prawn mixture between the pockets and top with the yogurt.

Tip

The filling works equally well in a tortilla wrap or on chunky seeded bread.

NOTES

Calories	Fibre	Salt	Sugar	Fat
333	3.8g	2.7g	0g	6.7g of which 3.5g is saturated

Scan QR Code
for an ingredients
shopping list

CHICKEN, LEMON & CHIVE EGG ROLLS WITH PEA HUMMUS

Serves 4   Preparation 20 minutes plus cooling   Cooking 15–20 minutes

Eggs 4

Unwaxed lemon 1 small, finely grated zest

Chives small bunch, chopped

Vegetable oil 2 tsp

Mayonnaise 4 tbsp

Cooked chicken 175g (6oz), thinly sliced

Cucumber ½, cut into thin strips

For the pea hummus

Frozen peas 100g (3½oz)

Garlic 1 clove, peeled

Sesame oil 2 tsp

Salt and freshly ground black pepper

First make the pea hummus. Cook the peas with the garlic in lightly salted boiling water for 4–5 minutes until tender. Drain well, reserving the cooking water. Cool for 10 minutes. Put the peas and garlic in a blender or food processor. Add 3 tablespoons reserved cooking water and the sesame oil. Blend for a few seconds until smooth and creamy. Season to taste and leave to cool.

Meanwhile, beat the eggs in a jug with the lemon zest, chives, 2 tablespoons water and seasoning. Brush a small non-stick frying pan with a little of the oil and place over a medium heat until hot. Pour in a quarter of the egg mixture and cook gently for about 2 minutes until set. Turn over and cook for a further minute until just cooked. Transfer to a wire rack covered with baking paper. Repeat with the remaining egg mixture to make four omelettes, stirring the mixture before pouring, and brushing the pan with a little more oil if necessary. When cool, stack between layers of baking paper, cover and chill until required.

To assemble, spread each omelette with 1 tablespoon mayonnaise, then spread with pea hummus. Arrange a layer of chicken and cucumber over each. Roll up tightly, wrap in cling film and chill until ready to serve. Cut in half for easy eating.

Tip

To make this suitable for vegetarians, swap the chicken for Quorn pieces or for tofu.

NOTES

Calories	Fibre	Salt	Sugar	Fat
451	2.1g	0.6g	0g	38.5g of which 4.3g is saturated

CHICKEN, ALMOND & BASIL SANDWICHES

Serves 2   Preparation 5 minutes   Cooking 20 minutes

Skinless chicken breast 1 large
Light mayonnaise 2 tbsp
Harissa paste 1 tsp
Ciabatta rolls 2
Rocket 15g (½oz)
Chopped basil 3 tbsp
Almonds 2 tbsp, halved

Place the chicken breast in a pan of boiling water, put on the lid and remove from the heat. Leave to poach for about 20 minutes until cooked through. Leave to cool completely.

In a small bowl mix the mayonnaise with the harissa.

Drain and slice the chicken. Split the rolls in half and spread the bottom halves with some of the harissa mayonnaise. Fill with rocket leaves, chicken, basil and almonds. Top with the remaining harissa mayonnaise and serve.

Tip

These are also delicious served warm: no need to leave the chicken to cool. Heat the rolls in the oven at 200°C/180°fan/Gas 6 for 8–10 minutes or according to the pack's instructions.

NOTES

Calories	Fibre	Salt	Sugar	Fat
581	3.1g	1g	0g	27.1g of which 3.2g is saturated

Scan QR Code
for an ingredients
shopping list

CORONATION CHICKEN WRAPS

Serves 2   Preparation 5 minutes

Cooked chicken tikka breast slices 160g pack, chopped
Raisins 2 tbsp
Mayonnaise 2 tbsp
Little Gem lettuce 1, trimmed and sliced
Tortilla wraps 2

Mix the chicken with the raisins and mayonnaise.
Scatter the lettuce over the wraps and top with the chicken mixture. Fold the ends in and then roll up. Cut each wrap in half and serve.

Tip
Use leftover roast chicken instead of the chicken tikka and mix a little curry powder into the mayonnaise instead.

NOTES

Calories	Fibre	Salt	Sugar	Fat
634	4.5g	1g	0g	28.9g of which 3.1g is saturated

AFTERNOON SNACKS

SUPER SEED OATY CRISPS

Makes 8–10 pieces   Preparation 20 minutes plus standing and cooling   Cooking 40 minutes

Coarse oatmeal 75g (3oz)

Assorted seeds 150g (5oz) – see Tip

Cornflour 2 tbsp

Salt ¾ tsp

Dried rosemary 1½ tsp

Olive oil 1 tbsp

Put all the ingredients in a large bowl and mix well. Gradually stir in 6 tablespoons warm water to make a crumbly mixture. Leave to stand for 15 minutes, then squeeze the ingredients together with your hands to make a ball. Add a little more water if the mixture is still a bit dry.

Preheat the oven to 190°C/170°fan/Gas 5.

Line a large baking tray with baking paper. Put the mix onto the lined tray and flatten, using your hands.

Place another sheet of baking paper on top and roll using a rolling pin to make a rough rectangle approx. 34 x 25cm (13 x 10in). The thinner you are able to roll the mixture, the crisper the biscuits. Remove the top layer of paper.

Bake for 20 minutes until lightly browned around the edges. Place a sheet of baking paper on the surface, lay another baking tray on top and carefully flip the trays over. Peel away the top paper and return to the oven for a further 20 minutes until crisp and lightly golden all over. Leave to cool for 10 minutes then slide onto a wire rack to cool completely. When cold, transfer to a board and break into pieces. Store in an airtight container.

Tip

Many supermarkets and health food shops sell pots of mixed seeds for snacking. These may include chia, flax, sesame and pumpkin seeds and are useful if you don't want to buy lots of different packets.

NOTES

Calories	Fibre	Salt	Sugar	Fat
83	1.2g	0.4g	0g	6.9g of which 1g is saturated

Scan QR Code for an ingredients shopping list

ROAST BEETROOT & FETA DIP

Serves 4–6   Preparation 15 minutes plus cooling   Cooking 1 hour

Raw beetroot 1 bunch (approx. 500g/1lb 2oz)

Cooked or drained canned cannellini beans 75g (3oz)

Dried chilli flakes or cumin seeds ¼ tsp

Feta cheese 65g (2½oz), chopped

Soured cream 4–6 tbsp

Salt and freshly ground black pepper

Mixed seeds 2 tsp (optional)

Breadsticks, carrot batons or Oaty Crisps (p44) to serve

Preheat the oven to 220°C/200°fan/Gas 7.

Roast the beetroot for about 1 hour or until tender. Leave to cool a little then top and tail, and peel away the skins.

Place the beetroot in a food processor with the beans, chilli flakes or cumin seeds, and 50g (2oz) of the Feta cheese. Whizz to blend together then whizz in enough soured cream to make a smooth dip. Season to taste.

Spoon into a bowl and top with the remaining Feta and mixed seeds, if using. Serve with breadsticks, carrot batons and/or Oaty Crisps.

Tips

Wear rubber gloves when peeling the beetroot to avoid staining your hands. Chilli flakes give a slight 'kick' to the dip, the cumin is more fragrant; choose your preference.

NOTES

Calories	Fibre	Salt	Sugar	Fat
101	2.9g	0.4g	0g	5.7g of which 3.6g is saturated

CHEESY PITTA CRISPS

Makes 36   Preparation 5 minutes   Cooking 15 minutes

Pitta breads 3
Dried sage 1½ tsp
Dried thyme 1½ tsp
Salt and freshly ground black pepper
Red Leicester cheese 75g (3oz), grated
Monterey Jack cheese 75g (3oz), grated

Preheat the oven to 190°C/170°fan/Gas 5. Line two baking sheets with baking paper.

Cut each pitta bread into six triangles and then split into thin halves. Place on baking sheets. Sprinkle the herbs over the pitta pieces and season to taste, then sprinkle over the cheeses.

Bake for 12–15 minutes until golden.

Tip

Instead of Monterey Jack use Cheddar or 25g (1oz) Parmesan.

NOTES

Calories	Fibre	Salt	Sugar	Fat
31	0.2g	0.2g	0g	1.3g of which 0.8g is saturated

Scan QR Code
for an ingredients
shopping list

CHORIZO & COURGETTE 'MUFFINS'

Serves 3   Preparation 10 minutes   Cooking 25 minutes

Butter for greasing
Courgette 1 (approx. 125g/4½oz), coarsely grated
Spring onions 2, trimmed and finely sliced
Thinly sliced chorizo 12 slices (50g/2oz), cut into fine strips
Ready-grated Cheddar and Mozzarella mix 50g (2oz)
Eggs 6
Salt and freshly ground black pepper

Preheat the oven to 180°C/160°fan/Gas 4. Generously butter a six-hole muffin tin.

Pat the courgette dry on kitchen paper, then divide the courgette, spring onions, chorizo and then the cheese between the muffin tins.

In a large jug, whisk the eggs well, adding plenty of seasoning. Pour into the muffin tins then carefully place in the oven and bake for 25 minutes or until the muffins are risen and golden.

Leave in the tins for 5 minutes then slide a knife round each one and turn them out.

Tip
If you don't want to weigh the cheese it works out at 1 tablespoon per muffin.

NOTES

Calories	Fibre	Salt	Sugar	Fat
313	1g	1.9g	0g	23.7g of which 9.8g is saturated

BERRIES WITH PASSION

Serves 2   Preparation 5 minutes

Strawberries 50g (2oz), hulled and halved or sliced if large

Raspberries 50g (2oz)

Blueberries 50g (2oz)

Fresh coconut flesh 50g (2oz), cut into small chunks or grated

Passion fruit 1, halved

Dark chocolate with sea salt 2 squares (15g/½oz)

Arrange the berries and coconut on a platter to share or in two shallow bowls. Scoop out the passion fruit and add to the berries.

Using a swivel head potato peeler, shave the chocolate into small curls over the fruit. Serve immediately or chill in the fridge until ready to serve.

Tips

Serve with yogurt, drizzled with honey, if you like. The fruits and coconut could be layered up in a tumbler with a scoop of mango or strawberry sorbet on top.

NOTES

Calories	Fibre	Salt	Sugar	Fat
88	5g	0.5g	4.7g	10.8g of which 8.7g is saturated

Scan QR Code
for an ingredients
shopping list

DATE & SPELT SCONE

Serves 6   Preparation 15 minutes   Cooking 25 minutes

Pitted Deglet Nour dates 110g (4oz)

Light spelt flour 125g (4½oz)

Baking powder 2 tsp

Green cardamom pods 16, husks removed, roughly ground using a pestle and mortar to make 1 tsp ground cardamom

Salt pinch

Butter 25g (1oz), cold and cut into slivers

Clear honey 2 tsp

Buttermilk or natural yogurt 5 tbsp

Egg 1, beaten

Porridge oats 1 tbsp

To serve

Butter 75g (3oz)

Orange ½, grated zest

Using scissors, snip the dates into small pieces into a bowl. Pour over 100ml (3½fl oz) hot water and leave to soak for 10 minutes.

Preheat the oven to 200°C/180°fan/Gas 6. Line a baking sheet with baking paper.

Mix the flour, baking powder, ½ teaspoon of the ground cardamom and a pinch of salt in a large bowl. Using your fingertips, rub in the butter. Stir in the honey, buttermilk or yogurt and drained dates. Mix lightly to a soft scone dough.

Turn the dough out onto the lined baking sheet and shape into a round approx. 15cm (6in) in diameter. Cut the scone almost through into six portions.

Brush the egg over the top and sides (you will not need it all) then sprinkle the oats over and pat gently to help them stick. Bake for 25 minutes.

Meanwhile, to serve, soften the butter and mix in the orange zest and remaining ½ teaspoon of cardamom. Put in a small pot.

Cool the scone on a wire rack. Break into six pieces, split and serve warm with the flavoured orange butter.

Tips

The scone will keep for 3 days in an airtight container. It is best served warm so pop it in the microwave for a few seconds. It will freeze for a month and the butter can also be frozen, wrapped in baking paper.

NOTES

Calories	Fibre	Salt	Sugar	Fat
253	2.8g	0.4g	1.9g	15.4g of which 9.1g is saturated

CHOCOLATE & WALNUT BANANA BREAD

Serves 8–10   Preparation 15 minutes   Cooking 1 hour 10 minutes

Butter for greasing

Ripe bananas 4 (approx. 375–400g/13–14oz peeled weight), plus 1 extra banana to decorate

Eggs 3

Light muscovado sugar 200g (7oz)

Vanilla extract 1 tsp

Butter 110g (4oz), melted

Self-raising flour 225g (8oz)

Ground cinnamon 1 tsp

Dark chocolate 100g (3½oz), roughly chopped

Walnut pieces 75g (3oz), roughly chopped

Preheat the oven to 180°C/160°fan/Gas 4. Butter a 900g (2lb) loaf tin and put a strip of baking paper along the length and up over the short sides of the tin.

Mash the bananas roughly in a large bowl. Add the eggs, sugar, vanilla and butter and beat well. Stir in the flour and cinnamon and mix until just combined then gently fold in the chocolate and nuts.

Pour the mixture into the tin. Peel the extra banana, slice lengthways and arrange cut side up on top. Bake for 1 hour to 1 hour 10 minutes until a skewer inserted into the centre comes out clean. Leave in the tin to cool for 10 minutes before lifting out onto a wire rack to cool.

Tips

A perfect recipe for using up ripe bananas, which are naturally sweet. Don't overwork the mixture. Use chocolate chips instead of chopped chocolate if you prefer.

NOTES

Calories	Fibre	Salt	Sugar	Fat
395	2.3g	0.3g	25.5g	19g of which 8.5g is saturated

Scan QR Code
for an ingredients
shopping list

MANGO & CRANBERRY BREAD PUDDING

Makes 12 slices   Preparation 15 minutes plus cooling   Cooking 30–35 minutes

Butter for greasing

Ground cinnamon 2 tsp

Eggs 2, beaten

Milk 300ml (½ pint)

Wholemeal bread 300g (11oz), any tough crusts removed, then cubed

Ready-to-eat dried mango 65g (2½oz), chopped

Ready-to-eat dried cranberries 3 tbsp

Sultanas 75g (3oz)

Granulated sugar 2 tbsp

Preheat the oven to 190°C/170°fan/Gas 5. Butter a square dish or tin approximately 23 x 23cm (9 x 9in).

In a mixing bowl, stir the cinnamon and eggs into the milk. Add the bread, mix well and leave to soak for 5 minutes.

Stir in the dried fruit and 1 tablespoon sugar then press into the prepared tin. Sprinkle with the remaining sugar.

Bake for 30–35 minutes until set. Leave in the tin to cool. When cold cut into 12 slices and store in an airtight container.

Tips

If using sliced bread, the crusts are soft enough to be left on. Only remove tough or dark crusts, which may affect the texture or flavour. Use any combination of dried fruit you like.

NOTES

Calories	Fibre	Salt	Sugar	Fat
155	2.8g	0.4g	3.3g	2.7g of which 1.1g is saturated

OATY MELTING MOMENTS

Makes 24   Preparation 20 minutes   Cooking 15–20 minutes

Butter 110g (4oz), softened
Caster sugar 75g (3oz)
Egg yolk 1
Vanilla extract a few drops
Self-raising flour 150g (5oz)
Rolled oats 25g (1oz)

Preheat the oven to 190°C/170°fan/Gas 5 and grease two baking sheets.

Cream together the butter and sugar until pale and fluffy, then beat in the egg yolk and vanilla extract.

Stir in the flour to give a soft dough, knead until smooth, then divide into 24 portions. Form each portion into a ball, then gently roll in the oats.

Place on the baking sheets and bake for 15–20 minutes until golden.

Cool slightly before transferring to a wire rack to cool completely.

Tip

Add some finely grated lemon zest for a little tang.

NOTES

Calories	Fibre	Salt	Sugar	Fat
75	0.3g	0.1g	3.1g	4.2g of which 2.5g is saturated

Scan QR Code
for an ingredients
shopping list

NUTTY CACAO TREATS

Makes 26–30   Preparation 30 minutes plus chilling   (F)

Mixed nuts of your choice 110g (4oz)
No added sugar peanut butter 280g jar
Pitted dates 110g (4oz), roughly chopped
Unsweetened desiccated coconut 110g (4oz)
Ground almonds 110g (4oz)
Cacao powder 50g (2oz)
Clear honey or agave nectar 2 tbsp

Place the nuts into a food processor and pulse until chopped. Add all the remaining ingredients and pulse until mixed together. If the mixture is too dry (this depends on how sticky the dates are), add a little more honey or agave nectar.

Form into about 30 balls the size of walnuts. Place in the freezer for 30 minutes to firm up.

Transfer the cacao balls to the fridge (leaving some in the freezer, if you like).

Tips

Cacao powder is available from health food shops. These will keep, chilled, for about a week. Use either smooth or crunchy peanut butter, dependent on your preference.

NOTES

Calories	Fibre	Salt	Sugar	Fat
142	1.8g	0.1g	1.2g	11.3g of which 3.8g is saturated

WEEKDAY MEALS

HOT ROAST ASPARAGUS & POTATO SALAD

Serves 4   Preparation 5 minutes   Cooking 25 minutes

Baby new potatoes 450g (1lb), scrubbed

Olive oil 4 tbsp

Salt and freshly ground black pepper

Asparagus spears 250–350g (9–12oz)

Lean back bacon rashers 4, trimmed and cut into thin strips

Lemon juice 3 tbsp

Clear honey 1 tbsp

Wholegrain mustard 1 tbsp

Celery sticks 4, chopped

Leek 1 small, trimmed and finely shredded

Watercress 25g (1oz)

Preheat the oven to 220°C/200°fan/Gas 7.

Halve the potatoes and place in a bowl. Toss in 2 tablespoons olive oil. Spread the potatoes on a large baking tray and season with salt and pepper. Bake for 10 minutes.

Meanwhile, trim about 2.5cm (1in) from the woody ends of the asparagus and cut each spear in half. Toss the asparagus and bacon with the potatoes. Return to the oven and bake for a further 15 minutes until the potatoes are lightly golden and tender.

Mix the remaining oil with the lemon juice, honey and mustard.

To serve, drain the roasted vegetables and bacon. Mix the celery, leek and watercress together then pile onto serving plates and top with the hot vegetables and bacon. Drizzle with the dressing and serve immediately.

Tips

Instead of bacon you could use smoked salmon, cooked chicken or grated cheese – just add to the roasted asparagus and potatoes to serve. This salad is equally delicious if the roasted vegetables are left to cool then mixed with the other ingredients and served as a cold salad.

NOTES

Calories	Fibre	Salt	Sugar	Fat
275	5.3g	1.4g	4.6g	16g of which 3.2g is saturated

Scan QR Code for an ingredients shopping list

WARM CARROT, KALE & CASHEW SALAD WITH MISO DRESSING

Serves 2   Preparation 5 minutes   Cooking 16 minutes

Carrots 2–3, peeled and cut into thin batons
Olive oil 2 tbsp
Prepared kale 65g (2½oz)
Cashew nuts 50g (2oz)
Miso Easy Traditional 1 sachet
Rice wine vinegar 2 tsp
Dessert apple 1 small, cored and cut into thin batons

Preheat the oven to 200°C/180°fan/Gas 6.

Mix the carrots with 1 tablespoon of the olive oil and scatter in a large roasting tin. Roast for 8 minutes.

Add the kale and cashew nuts to the tin and mix together. Roast for a further 5–8 minutes until the carrots are tender and the kale is crisp.

Whisk the miso with the vinegar and the remaining oil to make a dressing.

Remove the vegetables from the oven. Add the apple and dressing, mix well and serve.

Tips

Miso Easy Traditional is a Japanese soybean paste used for soups, marinades and dressings; you can find it in the Asian section of the supermarket. Add a few cubes of Cheddar or Feta cheese, if you like.

NOTES

Calories	Fibre	Salt	Sugar	Fat
324	7.1g	0.8g	0g	24.6g of which 4.2g is saturated

BUTTERNUT SQUASH SUPER SALAD

Serves 2   Preparation 10 minutes   Cooking 20 minutes

Butternut squash 225g (8oz), peeled and cubed

Green lentils 75g (3oz), rinsed

Green beans 50g (2oz), trimmed and halved

Extra virgin olive oil 1 tbsp

Cider vinegar ½ tbsp

Salt and freshly ground black pepper

Baby salad leaves 40g (1½oz)

Chopped fresh mint 2 tbsp

Goat's cheese 50g (2oz), torn (optional)

Put the squash and lentils in a saucepan, cover with cold water and bring to the boil. Cover and simmer gently for 15 minutes.

Add the green beans and cook for a further 5 minutes or until the vegetables have softened. Drain and leave to cool slightly.

Mix the oil with the vinegar and season to taste.

Divide the salad leaves between two salad bowls, top with the lentils, squash, beans, chopped mint and cheese and drizzle with the dressing.

Tips

Use sweet potato instead of squash if you prefer. For a vegan dish omit the goat's cheese.

NOTES

Calories	Fibre	Salt	Sugar	Fat
296	8.3g	1.4g	0g	13.1g of which 5.4g is saturated

Scan QR Code
for an ingredients
shopping list

BEETROOT FRITTERS WITH SPINACH & BEAN SALAD

Serves 2   Preparation 15 minutes   Cooking 10 minutes

Raw beetroot approx. 200g (7oz), well scrubbed

Frozen edamame beans 150g (5oz)

Spring onions 2, trimmed and finely sliced

Ground cumin ½ tsp

Chopped fresh tarragon or dill leaves 1 good tbsp

Salt and freshly ground black pepper

Plain flour 4 tbsp

Eggs 2, beaten

Olive oil 3 tbsp

Spinach leaves 75g (3oz)

Toasted chopped walnuts 1 tbsp

Balsamic vinegar 2 tsp

Greek yogurt 4 tbsp

Hot horseradish sauce 1 tbsp

Grate the beetroot. Set aside on a plate lined with kitchen paper and put another piece of paper on top.

Cook the beans in simmering water for 3 minutes, then drain, refresh in cold water and drain.

In a large bowl, mix the spring onions, cumin, tarragon or dill, salt and pepper and grated beetroot. Sprinkle the flour over then mix it in well and stir in the beaten eggs.

Heat 2 tablespoons oil in a large frying pan and put in 6 generous tablespoons of the mixture. Fry for 2–3 minutes on each side then drain on kitchen paper.

To serve, put the spinach leaves on two plates, scatter the beans and nuts over and drizzle with the remaining oil and the balsamic vinegar. Place the fritters on the plates. Mix the yogurt with the horseradish in a small bowl and serve on the side.

Tips

Wear rubber gloves when grating the beetroot so you don't get pink fingers but watch you don't grate the glove! Fresh or frozen broad beans or peas can be used instead of edamame. Fry the fritters in two batches if your pan is not very big.

NOTES

Calories	Fibre	Salt	Sugar	Fat
739	12g	1.7g	0g	46.9g of which 11.9g is saturated

SPICED SWEET POTATO SOUP

Serves 4   Preparation 10 minutes   Cooking 30 minutes

Butter 15g (½oz)

Onion 1, peeled and sliced

Sweet potato 1 large, peeled and cut into even-sized chunks

Parsnip 1, peeled and sliced

Swede 175g (6oz), peeled and diced

Balti paste 1 tbsp

Vegetable stock 900ml (1½ pints)

Salt and freshly ground black pepper

Crème fraîche and naan bread to serve (optional)

In a large saucepan melt the butter over a low heat and add the onion. Cover and sweat for 5 minutes or until soft.

Increase the heat slightly and add the vegetables and balti paste. Cook, stirring, for 2 minutes. Stir in 800ml (28fl oz) stock and bring to the boil. Simmer for 20 minutes or until the vegetables are soft.

Remove from the heat, purée with a stick blender, add a little more stock if needed, and season to taste.

Top with a spoonful of crème fraîche if you like and serve with naan bread.

Tip

Use any type of curry paste that you have available. Scatter with chopped Feta cheese before serving, if you like.

NOTES

Calories	Fibre	Salt	Sugar	Fat
126	5.3g	1.5g	0g	5.3g of which 2.1g is saturated

Scan QR Code
for an ingredients
shopping list

PORTOBELLO BURGERS

Serves 4   Preparation 10 minutes   Cooking 20 minutes

Large Portobello mushrooms 4

Cooked brown rice 100g (3½oz)

Cooked beetroot in natural juice 100g (3½oz), drained

Pesto sauce 50g (2oz)

Salt and freshly ground black pepper

Red cabbage 200g (7oz), finely sliced

Chopped fresh chives 2 tbsp

Mayonnaise 75g (3oz)

Wholegrain rolls 4 large, halved

Baby salad leaves 50g (2oz)

Preheat the oven to 220°C/200°fan/Gas 7.

Wipe the mushrooms. Remove the stalks and chop. Mix the stalks with the rice. Grate the beetroot, blot with kitchen paper to remove excess juice, and mix into the rice along with the pesto sauce. Spoon into the mushrooms.

Place the mushrooms, side by side, in a shallow baking dish. Season well. Pour 150ml (¼ pint) boiling water into the dish, cover with foil and bake for 10 minutes. Uncover and cook for a further 10 minutes until tender.

Meanwhile, put the cabbage in a bowl and mix in the chives and mayonnaise. Cover and chill until required.

To serve, drain the mushrooms and place in the rolls. Top with the red cabbage slaw and baby leaves then the top halves of the rolls. Serve immediately.

Tip

Check that the pesto is suitable for vegetarians, as pesto is traditionally made with Parmesan cheese, which is made from animal rennet.

NOTES

Calories	Fibre	Salt	Sugar	Fat
374	7g	1.5g	0g	20.6g of which 2.2g is saturated

WINTER VEG CURRY WITH PICKLE & NAAN BREAD

Serves 4   Preparation 30 minutes plus rising   Cooking 35 minutes

Olive oil 1 tbsp

Onion 1, peeled and chopped

Curry paste 3 tbsp

Potatoes 400g (14oz), peeled & cubed

Squash 400g (14oz), peeled & cubed

Milk 350ml (12fl oz)

Vegetable stock 300ml (½ pint)

Tomato purée 1 tbsp

Redcurrant jelly 1 tbsp

Cauliflower 400g (14oz), cut into florets

Chopped fresh coriander 3 tbsp

For the naan bread

Strong white flour 225g (8oz)

Salt ¼ tsp

Caster sugar ½ tsp

Fast-action dried yeast 1 tsp

Butter 15g (½oz), melted

Warm milk approx. 100ml (3½fl oz)

Olive oil 1 tbsp

For the pickle

Carrot 1 large, cut into ribbons with a peeler

Courgette 1, cut into ribbons

Rice vinegar 1 tbsp

Salt and freshly ground black pepper

To make the naan bread, sift the flour, salt and sugar into a mixing bowl. Add the yeast and mix together. Make a well in the centre and add the butter and enough warm milk to make a soft but not sticky dough. Knead for 5–10 minutes until smooth, cover and leave in a warm place for about an hour until doubled in size.

Make the pickle: mix the carrot and courgette ribbons with the rice vinegar and season.

Divide the naan dough into four balls then roll into teardrop shapes about 5mm (¼in) thick. Cover with oiled clingfilm and leave to rise for about 20 minutes.

To make the curry, heat the oil in a large saucepan and fry the onion for 5 minutes until softened. Add the curry paste and stir for 2 minutes.

Add the potatoes and squash with the milk, stock, tomato purée and redcurrant jelly. Bring to the boil, then simmer gently for 10 minutes.

Add the cauliflower and cook for a further 5 minutes or until the vegetables are just tender. Sprinkle with coriander. Preheat the grill to hot.

Brush the naan with oil and grill for 3–4 minutes on each side. Serve with the curry and pickle.

Calories	Fibre	Salt	Sugar	Fat
550	11.1g	1.8g	0g	15g of which 4.3g is saturated

Scan QR Code for an ingredients shopping list

CAULIFLOWER BIRIYANI WITH SWEET CARROT RELISH

Serves 4   Preparation 10 minutes   Cooking 25 minutes

Sunflower oil 1 tbsp

Onion 1, peeled and thinly sliced

Mild curry powder 1 tbsp

Cardamom pods 6, split

Bay leaves 2

Basmati rice 175g (6oz), rinsed

Red lentils 50g (2oz), rinsed

Vegetable stock 600ml (1 pint)

Salt 1 tsp

Cauliflower 1, cut into large florets

Fresh coriander small bunch, roughly chopped

For the carrot relish

Carrot 1 large, peeled and grated

Sultanas 50g (2oz)

Roast cashew nuts 50g (2oz), crushed

White wine vinegar 4 tsp

Clear honey 1 tbsp (omit if vegan)

Black onion seeds 1 tsp (optional)

Heat the oil in a large saucepan and gently fry the onion, stirring, for about 5 minutes until softened but not browned.

Add the curry powder, cardamom pods, bay leaves, rice and lentils and cook, stirring, for a further minute. Add the stock and salt and bring to the boil. Add the cauliflower, cover and simmer gently for about 15 minutes, stirring occasionally, until the rice and cauliflower are just tender. Remove from the heat, cover and leave for 5 minutes. Discard the bay leaves and cardamom pods.

Meanwhile, make the relish. Place the carrot in a bowl and stir in the sultanas and cashew nuts then stir in the vinegar, honey and onion seeds, if using. Cover and chill until ready to serve.

To serve, pile the cauliflower rice onto warm serving plates, sprinkle with coriander and serve with the carrot relish.

Tip

Keep the cauliflower pieces quite large so that the rice and lentils cook thoroughly and the cauliflower retains some texture.

NOTES

Calories	Fibre	Salt	Sugar	Fat
405	6.7g	1.9g	4.5g	10.8g of which 1.8g is saturated

BROCCOLI PENNE WITH ALMOND PESTO

Serves 4   Preparation 10 minutes   Cooking 10 minutes

Penne pasta 300g (11oz)
Broccoli 200g (7oz), broken into florets
Capers 2 tbsp, rinsed
Chilli flakes ½–1 tsp (optional)

For the almond pesto
Whole blanched almonds 25g (1oz)
Garlic 1 clove, peeled and chopped
Basil leaves 25g (1oz)
Olive oil 3 tbsp
Parmesan cheese 50g (2oz), finely grated
Salt and freshly ground black pepper

Cook the pasta in a large saucepan of salted boiling water for 5 minutes.

Add the broccoli and cook for 5 minutes more.

To make the pesto, put the almonds, garlic, basil and olive oil into a big jug and use a stick blender to make the pesto. Stir in half the Parmesan and season to taste.

Drain the pasta and broccoli, reserving a little of the cooking water. Tip back into the pan and stir in the pesto.

Spoon into four warm bowls. Scatter with capers, chilli flakes if using, and the remaining Parmesan and cooking water.

Tip

If cooking for a vegetarian, use an Italian-style vegetarian hard cheese instead of Parmesan, which is made with animal rennet.

NOTES

Calories	Fibre	Salt	Sugar	Fat
442	5.8g	0.7g	0g	17g of which 4.1g is saturated

Scan QR Code
for an ingredients
shopping list

ROASTED COD LOIN WRAPPED IN PANCETTA

Serves 2 Preparation 10 minutes   Cooking 25 minutes

Cod loin 2 pieces, 150–175g (5–6oz) each

Smoked sliced pancetta 8–10 slices, weighing about 50g (2oz)

Olive oil 2 tbsp

Salt and freshly ground black pepper

Asparagus tips 125g (4½oz), trimmed

Ready-to-eat mixed grains 250g packet

Light mayonnaise 2–3 tbsp

Lime ½–1, juice only

Preheat the oven to 200°C/180° fan/Gas 6. Generously wrap the cod loins in pancetta. Drizzle a little oil in a roasting tin and pop the cod loins on top of the oil. Drizzle the loins with a little more oil, season with pepper and roast in the oven for 10 minutes.

Meanwhile, coat the asparagus in the remaining oil and season with salt and pepper.

Remove the cod loins from the oven, baste the pancetta with the juices in the pan and add the asparagus, making sure they are in a single layer. Roast for a further 8–10 minutes until the cod loins are cooked through and the asparagus is tender.

Heat the mixed grains in the microwave according to the packet's instructions. Flavour the mayonnaise with lime juice, adding it gradually so it doesn't split, and season with salt and pepper.

To serve, set a spoonful of mixed grains on each plate, pop the cod loin on top and arrange the asparagus neatly to the side. Serve at once with the lime mayonnaise.

Tip

Use Parma ham instead of pancetta if you like. Ready-to-eat grains can be found in the couscous/rice aisle of the supermarket.

NOTES

Calories	Fibre	Salt	Sugar	Fat
640	5.4g	2.9g	0g	39.1g of which 8.7g is saturated

SALMON WITH ROAST RED PEPPER SALAD

Serves 2   Preparation 15 minutes   Cooking 15 minutes

Olive oil 2 tbsp

Lemon 1, juice only

Salt and freshly ground black pepper

Salmon fillets 2 (approx. 150g/5oz each)

Red pepper 1, deseeded and finely sliced

Red onion 1 small, peeled and thinly sliced

Garlic 1 clove, peeled and finely chopped

Chopped fresh parsley 1 tbsp

Lime and coriander basmati rice 250g pack

Preheat the oven to 220°C/200°fan/Gas 7. Line a roasting tin with foil.

Mix together 1 tablespoon oil and the lemon juice, then season well.

Place the salmon in the centre of the foil and drizzle with the oil mixture. Wrap tightly and bake for 15 minutes or until the salmon is cooked.

Meanwhile, in a separate roasting tin, toss the red pepper in the remaining oil, season, and roast for 15 minutes until just tender, turning occasionally.

Remove the pepper from the oven and tip into a bowl with the onion, garlic and parsley and season to taste.

Cook the rice according to the pack's instructions and serve with the salmon and salad.

Tip

If you prefer, cook the onion in the oven with the red pepper.

NOTES

Calories	Fibre	Salt	Sugar	Fat
569	2.2g	1.2g	0g	26.9g of which 4.9g is saturated

Scan QR Code
for an ingredients
shopping list

SARDINE & ROCKET SPAGHETTI

Serves 4 Preparation 5 minutes   Cooking 15 minutes

Spaghetti 250–300g (9–11oz)
Anchovy fillets in oil 50g can
Olive oil 1 tbsp
Garlic 1–2 cloves, peeled and crushed
Dried chilli flakes a pinch
Fresh white breadcrumbs 6 tbsp
Sardines in olive oil 120g can
Lemon 1, finely grated zest
Rocket 4 good handfuls (75g–110g/3–4oz)

Add the spaghetti to a large pan of boiling water and cook according to the pack's instructions.

Meanwhile, tip the anchovies with their oil into a large frying pan. Add the olive oil, garlic and chilli flakes and stir over a gentle heat for 1–2 minutes until mushy.

Turn up the heat, add the breadcrumbs and stir briskly until golden and crunchy. Tip onto kitchen paper.

Flake the sardines straight into the frying pan with their oil.

Drain the pasta, reserving some of the cooking water. Tip it into the frying pan with the lemon zest, a little pasta water and half the rocket. Toss together and then divide between four bowls. Sprinkle each portion with more rocket and the anchovy crumbs.

Tip

Add some halved black olives and a squeeze of lemon juice if you like.

NOTES

Calories	Fibre	Salt	Sugar	Fat
415	4.7g	2.3g	0g	9.9g of which 1.8g is saturated

SWEET CHILLI GRILLED MACKEREL SALAD

Serves 4   Preparation 20 minutes   Cooking 10 minutes

Prepared mango 200g (7oz), finely chopped

Red pepper 1, deseeded and chopped

Spring onions 4, trimmed and chopped

Carrot 1 large, peeled and coarsely grated

Mixed sprouting seeds 50g (2oz)

Fresh mackerel fillets 8 x 100g (3½oz)

Chinese five spice powder ½ tsp

Sweet chilli sauce 6 tbsp

Sesame oil 2 tsp

Sesame seeds 2 tbsp, lightly toasted

Crusty bread to serve (optional)

Put the mango in a bowl. Add the red pepper, spring onions and carrot and mix well. Toss in the sprouting seeds. Leave to one side.

Preheat the grill to medium–hot. Lightly season the mackerel fillets on both sides with five spice. Place the fillets on the grill rack, skin-side up, and cook for 4–5 minutes. Turn the fillets over and lightly brush with 2 tablespoons of the sweet chilli sauce. Cook for a further 5 minutes until cooked through. Drain the mackerel and flake away from the skin.

To serve, mix the remaining sweet chilli sauce with the sesame oil and mix into the salad. Arrange the salad on serving plates, top with warm flaked mackerel and sprinkle with sesame seeds. Serve immediately with crusty bread, if you like.

Tips

Sprouting seeds are a great source of vegetable protein. You will find packs of sprouts such as alfalfa, clover, broccoli and radish in the salad aisle in the supermarket. Replace with watercress if you prefer.

NOTES

Calories	Fibre	Salt	Sugar	Fat
693	6g	1g	1.2g	53.4g of which 10.7g is saturated

Scan QR Code
for an ingredients
shopping list

SPICED CHICKEN NOODLE SOUP

Serves 4–6 Preparation 15 minutes Cooking 40 minutes

Sunflower oil 2 tbsp

Shallots 2, peeled and sliced

Celery sticks 2, chopped

Garlic 3 cloves, peeled and sliced

Root ginger 5cm (2in) piece, peeled and chopped

Red chilli ½–1, deseeded and finely chopped

Chinese five spice stir-fry paste 2 tsp

Skinless chicken breasts 3

Lemongrass 2 sticks

Chicken stock 2 litres (3½ pints)

Dried rice noodles 125g (4½oz)

Spring onions 6, trimmed and sliced

Pak choi 3, trimmed and sliced

Chopped fresh coriander 2 tbsp

Heat the oil in a large saucepan and add the shallots, celery, garlic, half the ginger and half the chilli. Stir in the five spice paste and cook for 1 minute, stirring.

Add the chicken breasts and cook for 5 minutes, turning occasionally.

Add the lemongrass and pour in the stock. Bring to the boil then reduce the heat and simmer for 30 minutes.

Meanwhile, soak the noodles in boiling water for 3–5 minutes, then drain.

Remove the chicken from the stock and shred.

Strain the stock into another pan and add the noodles, chicken, spring onions, pak choi and the remaining ginger and chilli. Bring to the boil and simmer for 5 minutes until the pak choi is cooked. Serve scattered with coriander.

Tip

If pak choi is unavailable use spring cabbage.

NOTES

Calories	Fibre	Salt	Sugar	Fat
156	1.9g	0.2g	0g	4.9g of which 0.7g is saturated

CHICKEN & AVOCADO FAJITAS

Serves 3   Preparation 15 minutes   Cooking 5 minutes

Sunflower oil 1 tbsp

Paprika 1 tsp

Ground cumin ½ tsp

Ground coriander ½ tsp

Chilli powder ½ tsp

Lime 1, grated zest and juice

Mini chicken breast fillets 350g pack, cut into bite-sized pieces

Tortilla wraps 6

Cos lettuce ½, shredded

Avocado 1 large, peeled, stoned and sliced

Soured cream 4–6 tbsp (optional)

Chopped fresh coriander 2 tbsp

In a bowl mix together the oil, spices, lime zest and juice and use to coat the chicken.

Heat a non-stick frying pan and fry the chicken over a medium–high heat for about 5 minutes until cooked.

Warm the tortilla wraps according to the pack's instructions.

Divide the lettuce and avocado between the wraps, top with spiced chicken and soured cream, if using, sprinkle with coriander, roll up and serve.

Tip

For really speedy wraps buy ready-flavoured cooked chicken and omit the spices.

NOTES

Calories	Fibre	Salt	Sugar	Fat
621	8.5g	2.3g	0g	22.6g of which 6.1g is saturated

Scan QR Code
for an ingredients
shopping list

MASSAMAN THAI CHICKEN WITH NUTTY GREEN BEANS

Serves 2   Preparation 10 minutes plus marinating   Cooking 10 minutes

Chicken breasts 2 (about 300g/11oz), skin on

Massaman Thai curry paste 4 tsp

Thai sweet chilli sauce 4 tsp

Vegetable oil 2 tsp

Fine green beans 110g (4oz), trimmed

Lime 1, grated zest; juice from ½, the other ½ cut into wedges

Roughly chopped salted roasted peanuts 1 tbsp

Noodles or new potatoes to serve (optional)

Place the chicken breasts between two sheets of cling film and use a rolling pin to flatten them to approx. 1cm (½in) thick. Mix the curry paste with 2 teaspoons of the chilli sauce then rub this mixture over the chicken and set aside at room temperature for 10 minutes.

Meanwhile, heat a griddle pan until very hot. Put the chicken on the griddle and leave it for 3 minutes then turn it over and cook for another 3 minutes. Set aside on a warm plate.

Heat the oil in a wok or large frying pan and when hot, add the beans and stir-fry for 4 minutes until just tender and starting to char. Take off the heat, then add the lime zest, juice and nuts.

Divide the beans between two warm plates and drizzle with the remaining chilli sauce. Add the chicken and the lime wedges. Serve with noodles or new potatoes if you like.

Tip

The marinade will stick to the griddle pan so put that to soak as soon as you have finished cooking. This recipe is also good with lamb cutlets instead of chicken.

NOTES

Calories	Fibre	Salt	Sugar	Fat
377	3.7g	0.9g	0g	21.3g of which 2.3g is saturated

PAN-FRIED PORK WITH APPLE SLAW

Serves 2   Preparation 10 minutes   Cooking 25 minutes

Olive oil 2 tbsp, plus 1 tsp

Fresh sage leaves 8–10

Salt and freshly ground black pepper

Plain flour 1 tbsp

Pork tenderloin 250g (9oz), trimmed of fat and cut into 6 slices

Cloudy apple juice 150ml (¼ pint)

Pork stock 150ml (¼ pint)

Soy sauce 1 tbsp

Clear honey 1 tsp

Red cabbage 75g (3oz), finely shredded

Savoy cabbage 75g (3oz), finely shredded

Dessert apple 1, quartered, cored and cut into matchsticks

Crusty bread to serve (optional)

Heat 1 tablespoon olive oil in a large lidded frying pan and fry the sage leaves for 2–3 minutes until crisp. Drain on kitchen paper and set aside.

Season the flour and use to coat the pork slices. Heat another tablespoon of oil in the pan and fry the pork for about 4 minutes on each side until browned.

Pour the apple juice and stock into the pan and bring to the boil. Cover and simmer for about 10 minutes until the pork is cooked through. Remove the pork using a slotted spoon and keep warm. Boil the sauce for a couple of minutes to reduce slightly.

Meanwhile, whisk together the remaining 1 teaspoon oil, soy sauce and honey. Add the cabbage and apple, season with black pepper and toss everything together.

Serve the slaw with the pork and its sauce and garnish with the sage leaves. Add a slice of crusty bread, if you like.

Tip

Peel the apple if you like, or keep the skin on, or use a pear instead.

NOTES

Calories	Fibre	Salt	Sugar	Fat
422	3.7g	2.7g	3g	21g of which 4.3g is saturated

Scan QR Code for an ingredients shopping list

INDONESIAN-STYLE PORK NOODLE SALAD

Serves 4 Preparation 15 minutes Cooking 10 minutes

Dry rice stick noodles 200g (7oz)

Lean pork mince 500g (1lb 2oz)

Garlic 2 cloves, peeled and crushed

Root ginger 2cm (¾in) piece, peeled and grated

Spring onions 1 bunch, trimmed and chopped

Light soy sauce 3 tbsp

Limes 2

Clear honey 1 tbsp

Fresh coriander small bunch, roughly chopped

Fresh mint small bunch, roughly chopped

Red chilli 1, deseeded and finely chopped

Roast peanuts 50g (2oz), crushed

Carrot, radish and cucumber salad to serve (optional)

Put the noodles in a large heatproof bowl and cover with boiling water. Leave to soak for 5 minutes to soften, then drain well, cover and set aside.

Put the pork in a bowl and mix in the garlic, ginger, spring onions and 1 tablespoon soy sauce.

Heat a wok or large frying pan until hot. Add the pork mixture and dry fry over a high heat for 5 minutes, stirring to break up the meat into small clumps, until lightly browned all over.

Squeeze the juice from one of the limes and pour over the pork along with the remaining soy sauce and honey. Stir-fry for a further 3–4 minutes until cooked through.

To serve, stir the noodles through the pork then spoon into bowls and sprinkle with chopped herbs, chilli and peanuts. Cut the remaining lime into wedges and serve with the pork and noodles. Serve with a shredded carrot, radish and cucumber salad, if you like.

Tips

Dry rice noodles are an economical way of buying noodles. Look for them in the supermarket with other Asian groceries. Alternatively, use 600g (1lb 5oz) moist fresh rice noodles – heat as directed on the pack. To serve as a hot noodle dish, add the rehydrated noodles to the pork along with the lime juice and stir-fry for 3–4 minutes until piping hot.

NOTES

Calories	Fibre	Salt	Sugar	Fat
430	3g	2g	4.6g	18.9g of which 5.7g is saturated

PEA & BASIL SOUP WITH CHORIZO TOASTS

Serves 2 Preparation 5 minutes Cooking 15 minutes

Chorizo 40g (1½oz), chopped

Petits pois 300g (11oz)

Vegetable stock 450ml (¾ pint)

Baguette or small rustic loaf 2–4 slices

Cheddar cheese 25g (1oz)

Chopped basil 2 tbsp

Extra virgin olive oil 2 tsp, to serve

In a large saucepan fry 25g (1oz) of the chorizo for 2–4 minutes until its oil is released.

Reduce the heat, add the petits pois and stir for 2 minutes. Pour in the stock, bring to the boil then simmer for 10 minutes.

Meanwhile, preheat the grill and lightly toast the bread on one side. Mix the cheese with the remaining chorizo and pile onto the untoasted side of the bread. Grill for 4–7 minutes until the cheese is bubbling.

Add the basil to the soup. Whizz with a stick blender until smooth. Serve in warm bowls, with a swirl of olive oil and with the chorizo toasts.

Tip

For a vegetarian version omit the chorizo and fry the peas in butter instead. Serve with cheese on toast (minus the chorizo).

NOTES

Calories	Fibre	Salt	Sugar	Fat
374	8.9g	3.9g	0g	18.5g of which 6.6g is saturated

Scan QR Code for an ingredients shopping list

LAMB WITH ROASTED CAULIFLOWER

Serves 2 Preparation 15 minutes Cooking 12 minutes

Cauliflower 200g (7oz), cut into small florets

Red onion 1 small, peeled and finely chopped

Olive oil 3 tbsp

Ground cumin ¼ tsp

Ground turmeric ¼ tsp

Salt and freshly ground black pepper

Lamb cutlets or chops 4

Fresh parsley 10g (¼oz), finely chopped

Mint leaves 10g (¼ oz), finely chopped

Lemon ½, grated zest and juice

Ready-to-eat dried apricots 8, snipped into small pieces

Pomegranate seeds 4 tbsp (optional)

Tzatziki 110g (4oz) to serve

Preheat the oven to 200°C/180°fan/Gas 6.

Put the cauliflower and onion in a roasting tin, drizzle with 2 tablespoons of the oil, sprinkle with the spices and a little salt and pepper and stir. Roast for 8–10 minutes, stirring once, until just tender.

Meanwhile, heat a griddle pan. Brush the remaining oil over the lamb, season with salt and pepper and griddle for 3–5 minutes on each side, depending on thickness, then stand the cutlets on their edges for 2 minutes to cook the fatty skin. Cover the pan, take off the heat and leave to stand for 2 minutes.

Stir the parsley, mint, lemon zest and juice, apricots and pomegranate seeds, if using, into the roasted cauliflower. Spoon onto plates, top with the lamb and serve with spoonfuls of tzatziki.

Tips

Use ready-made tzatziki or make your own by mixing grated cucumber, chopped mint and lemon juice into Greek yogurt. Could be served with grilled chicken instead of lamb.

NOTES

Calories	Fibre	Salt	Sugar	Fat
687	5.2g	1.8g	0g	52.1g of which 19.4g is saturated

LEBANESE LENTILS WITH LAMB & CHARD

Serves 3–4   Preparation 10 minutes   Cooking 30 minutes

Green or brown lentils 110g (4oz), rinsed

Vegetable oil 3 tbsp

Onion 1 small, peeled and finely sliced

Plain flour 1 tbsp

Cooked lamb 200g (7oz), shredded

Cooked potato 150g (5oz), cut into small chunks

Cumin seeds 1 tbsp

Coriander seeds 1 tbsp

Ground turmeric ¼ tsp

Ground cinnamon 1 tsp

Basmati rice 110g (4oz)

Chard 110g (4oz), leaves separated, stems thinly sliced

Salt and freshly ground black pepper

Flatbreads to serve (optional)

For the garlic yogurt

Greek yogurt 200g (7oz)

Garlic 1 large clove, peeled and crushed

Fresh coriander approx. 25g (1oz), chopped

Lemon 1, juice from ½, the other ½ cut into wedges

Preheat the oven to low.

Put the lentils in a pan, cover with cold water and bring to the boil. Cover and simmer for 15 minutes until tender.

Meanwhile, heat the oil in a sauté pan. Toss the onion slices in the flour to coat them then cook in the hot oil for about 5 minutes until crisp and golden. Tip onto a plate lined with kitchen paper and keep warm in the oven.

Pour all but 1 tablespoon of the hot oil from the pan into a small bowl. Reheat the pan, add the shredded lamb and potato and fry for a few minutes until crispy. Add to the plate in the oven.

Heat the pan with another tablespoon of the oil, add the seeds and cook for a few seconds until fragrant then add the ground spices and rice, stirring well to coat it in the spices. Add the drained lentils and 300ml (½ pint) hot water. Bring to a simmer then cook gently for 10 minutes.

In a small bowl mix the yogurt with the garlic, 2 tablespoons chopped coriander and the lemon juice. Set aside.

Add the lamb and potato to the rice and lentils, along with the chard, season with salt and pepper, cover and cook for 5 minutes until the chard leaves have just wilted.

Take the pan off the heat. Stir in half of the crispy onions. Pile onto a serving plate. Scatter the remaining onions and coriander leaves over and serve with the garlic yogurt and the lemon wedges. Serve with warm flatbreads, if you like.

Calories	Fibre	Salt	Sugar	Fat
503	6.9g	0.8g	0g	23.1g of which 8g is saturated

Scan QR Code for an ingredients shopping list

ASIAN STEAK & CASHEW STIR-FRY

Serves 4   Preparation 10 minutes   Cooking 10 minutes

Aberdeen Angus frying steak 300g (11oz)

Chinese five spice powder ½ tsp

Soy sauce 1 tbsp

Savoy cabbage 1 small, cored and finely shredded

Cashew nuts 50g (2oz)

Vegetable oil 4 tsp

Root ginger 2.5cm (1in) piece, unpeeled, grated

Garlic 1 clove, peeled and grated

Shallot 1, peeled and sliced

Dried chilli flakes ½–1 tsp

Thai fish sauce 1 tbsp

Lime 1, juice only

Fresh coriander and mint leaves 25g (1oz), roughly chopped

Put the steak on a plate and sprinkle with five spice powder then drizzle with soy sauce.

Put the cabbage into a colander over a large saucepan and pour a kettleful of boiling water over it. Leave to drain.

Heat a wok or large frying pan. Add the cashews and toast for a few minutes, stirring, until just turning brown. Tip them out into a small dish.

Add 2 teaspoons of oil to the wok and put over a high heat. Add the steak, reserving the marinade. Sear the meat for 1 minute on each side then set aside on a plate and keep warm.

Put the pan back on the heat, add the remaining oil along with the ginger, garlic, shallot and chilli flakes. Stir-fry for 30 seconds then add the cabbage and stir-fry for 3 minutes until it starts to soften. Pour in the reserved marinade along with the fish sauce, lime juice and half the herbs.

Spoon the cabbage onto a serving platter. Cut the steak into strips and arrange it on top, spooning on the meat juices. Scatter with cashews and the remaining herbs.

Tips

This could be made with strips of chicken instead of steak. Use January King or Sweetheart cabbage for a change and roasted peanuts instead of cashews.

NOTES

Calories	Fibre	Salt	Sugar	Fat
303	3.2g	0.8g	0g	21.4g of which 3.4g is saturated

VENISON WITH MUSHROOM & BLACKBERRY SAUCE

Serves 4   Preparation 5 minutes   Cooking 30 minutes

Salt and freshly ground black pepper

Venison steaks 4 x 125g (4½oz)

Olive oil 2 tbsp

Red onion 1 small, peeled and thinly sliced

Chestnut mushrooms 200g (7oz), sliced

Fresh thyme a few sprigs

Blackberries 150g (5oz)

Ruby port 3 tbsp

Blackberry or raspberry vinegar 3 tbsp

Bramble or redcurrant jelly 2 tbsp

Mash and green vegetables to serve (optional)

Season the venison on both sides. Set aside.

Heat 1 tablespoon olive oil in a frying pan and gently fry the onion and mushrooms with the thyme for 10 minutes until softened.

Stir in the blackberries, port, vinegar and jelly, bring to the boil, cover and simmer gently for 5 minutes until softened. Turn off the heat. Keep covered.

Meanwhile, heat the remaining oil in another frying pan until hot. Add the venison steaks and cook over a medium heat for 4 minutes on each side – this will cook them to rare. Pour over the hot blackberry sauce, cover and cook over a low heat for 5 minutes.

Discard the thyme and serve with mashed potatoes and green vegetables, if you like.

Tip

This sauce also works well with beef, duck, pheasant and pork – adjust cooking times accordingly.

NOTES

Calories	Fibre	Salt	Sugar	Fat
245	2.6g	0.7g	6g	7.9g of which 1.8g is saturated

Scan QR Code
for an ingredients
shopping list

WEEKEND SPECIALS

ITALIAN-STYLE STUFFED PEPPERS

Serves 4   Preparation 15 minutes   Cooking 40 minutes

Bulgur wheat with white and red quinoa (ready mixed) 75g (3oz), rinsed

Vegetable Stock Pot (or stock cube) 1

Red and yellow peppers 4 large

Spring onions 4, trimmed and finely sliced

Garlic 2 cloves, peeled and chopped

Chickpeas 400g can, rinsed and drained

Fresh mint 2 tbsp chopped plus 12 mint leaves

Lemon 1, grated zest and juice from ½, the other ½ cut into wedges

Salt and freshly ground black pepper

Cherry tomatoes 12, halved

Feta cheese 110g (4oz), crumbled

Black or green olives 16, pitted

Extra virgin olive oil to serve

Preheat the oven to 200°C/180°fan/Gas 6. Put a roasting tin in the oven to heat up.

Tip the grain mixture into a pan with the Stock Pot (or crumbled stock cube) and 450ml (¾ pint) boiling water. Bring to the boil, cover and simmer for 10 minutes.

Meanwhile, slice the peppers in half lengthways and remove the seeds. Arrange them cut-side up in the roasting tin and roast for 10 minutes.

Take the grains off the heat (do not drain) and stir in the spring onions, garlic, chickpeas, chopped mint, lemon zest and juice. Season well and pile the mixture into the peppers.

Scatter tomato halves, crumbled feta and olives on top. Put back in the oven to roast for a further 20 minutes.

Serve warm or cold, scattered with torn mint leaves, with a generous amount of olive oil drizzled over and lemon wedges on the side.

Tips

If you can't find the bulgur and quinoa mixture, use quinoa on its own. You could add a large pinch of dried thyme to the grain mixture, then scatter the cooked peppers with fresh thyme leaves or chopped parsley instead of mint.

NOTES

Calories	Fibre	Salt	Sugar	Fat
277	8.7g	2.2g	0g	12.2g of which 4.6g is saturated

Scan QR Code for an ingredients shopping list

SPICY LAMB & DATE PILAF

Serves 4   Preparation 25 minutes plus salting and standing   Cooking 30 minutes

Aubergines 2 (500g/1lb 2oz), trimmed and cut into 2cm (¾in) thick slices

Salt

Olive oil 4 tbsp

Ground cumin 1 tbsp

Ground coriander 2 tsp

Ground cinnamon 2 tsp

Red onion 1 large, peeled and sliced

Garlic 2 cloves, peeled and crushed

Basmati rice 200g (7oz), rinsed

Chicken stock 600ml (1 pint)

Medjool dates 100g (3½oz), pitted and chopped

Baby spinach 150g (5oz)

Freshly ground black pepper

Lean lamb leg steaks 400g (14oz), trimmed and cut into thin slices

Chopped fresh coriander 2 tbsp

Cherry tomatoes 150g (5oz), quartered

Layer the aubergine slices in a colander, sprinkling the layers with salt, and set aside over a bowl for 30 minutes to drain. Rinse well and then pat dry with kitchen paper.

Heat 3 tablespoons of the olive oil in a large saucepan and gently fry the spices, onion and garlic for 5 minutes. Add the aubergine, mix well, cover, reduce the heat and cook for 10 minutes, stirring occasionally.

Add the rice and stir to coat in the onion mixture. Add the stock, bring to the boil and simmer gently for about 10 minutes until the rice is just tender. Turn off the heat and stir in the dates and spinach. Cover and leave to stand while you cook the lamb.

Season the lamb lightly. Heat the remaining oil in a frying pan and stir-fry the lamb for 5 minutes until browned and tender. Stir in the coriander and tomatoes, then mix into the rice. Cover and stand for a further 5 minutes before serving on warm plates.

Tips

Strips of beef or pork work well instead of the lamb – adjust cooking time accordingly. Replace the dates with sultanas, dried apricots or pitted prunes if you prefer.

NOTES

Calories	Fibre	Salt	Sugar	Fat
594	8.4g	1.5g	0g	25.1g of which 7.4g is saturated

BEAN & BROCCOLI BURRITOS

Serves 4   Preparation 20 minutes   Cooking 10 minutes

Sunflower oil 2 tbsp

Onion 1 small, peeled and finely chopped

Garlic 2 cloves, peeled and finely chopped

Cumin seeds 1 tsp

Black beans or borlotti beans in water 400g can, drained and rinsed

Smoked sweet paprika 2 tsp

Tenderstem broccoli 110g (4oz) – thin stems if possible, or thicker stems cut lengthways

Red and yellow peppers 1 of each, deseeded and cut into strips

Avocado 1, halved and stoned

Lime 1, juice only

Red chilli 1, deseeded and chopped

Tomatoes 2, quartered, deseeded, roughly chopped

Fresh coriander 25g (1oz), chopped

Soft white or wholewheat tortillas 8 medium

Mature Cheddar cheese 110g (4oz), grated (optional)

Heat 1 tablespoon oil in a large frying pan, add the onion and cook for a few minutes until it softens. Stir in the garlic and cumin seeds, cook for a few seconds then tip in the beans, sprinkle in the paprika and cook for 3 minutes.

Add 3 tablespoons of boiling water, take the pan off the heat and crush the mixture with a potato masher, adding a little extra boiling water if needed. Put in a dish, cover and keep warm.

Wash out the pan, add the remaining oil and put back on the heat. When hot, add the broccoli and pepper strips and stir-fry for 5 minutes. Put in a dish and keep warm.

Meanwhile, scoop the avocado flesh into a bowl, add the lime juice and mash with a fork to the consistency of guacamole, then stir in the chilli, tomatoes and coriander.

To serve, warm the tortillas in the frying pan or microwave. Spread a few tablespoons of the bean mixture onto each tortilla, then add some of the stir-fried veg, a dollop of guacamole and a sprinkling of cheese, if using. Roll them up tightly, tucking the ends in.

Tips

Roll up the tortillas in the kitchen or put all the fillings on the table for people to help themselves. Serve soured cream, yogurt or tzatziki as an additional filling if you like. For a vegan burrito omit the cheese.

NOTES

Calories	Fibre	Salt	Sugar	Fat
689	9.1g	2.6g	0g	26.2g of which 10.7g is saturated

Scan QR Code for an ingredients shopping list

NUTTY SEEDED VEGGIE BURGERS

Serves 4   Preparation 10 minutes plus chilling   Cooking 25 minutes

Bulgur wheat 50g (2oz)

Vegetable stock 300ml (½ pint)

Unsalted cashew nuts 50g (2oz)

Brazil nuts 50g (2oz)

Mixed seeds 50g (2oz)

Garlic 1 clove, peeled

Wholemeal bread 1 small slice, torn into pieces

Egg 1

Harissa paste 2 tsp

Miso paste 2 tsp (optional)

Salt and freshly ground black pepper

Sunflower oil 1–2 tbsp

Brioche buns, tomato slices and salad leaves to serve

Place the bulgur wheat in a saucepan with the vegetable stock and bring to the boil. Cover and simmer for 15 minutes. Drain well.

Place the nuts, seeds, garlic, bread, egg and harissa paste (and miso, if using) in a food processor and whizz to blend together.

Stir in the bulgur wheat and season to taste. Shape into four patties, cover and chill for 1 hour.

Heat the oil in a non-stick frying pan and cook the burgers for 4–5 minutes on each side until golden brown.

Serve in brioche buns with tomatoes and salad leaves.

Tips

If you're not keen on spice use just 1 teaspoon of harissa paste or omit it altogether. Miso paste can be found in the oriental section in the supermarket and adds a delicious savoury flavour to the burgers.

NOTES

Calories	Fibre	Salt	Sugar	Fat
589	5.2g	1.7g	8.3g	34.2g of which 10.8g is saturated

SLOW-ROASTED COD WITH PEPPERS & CAPERS

Serves 4   Preparation 25 minutes   Cooking 1 hour 15 minutes

Red, yellow or orange peppers 4, deseeded and cut into chunky slices

Red onions 2, peeled and thickly sliced

Olive oil 3 tbsp

Balsamic vinegar 2 tbsp

Salt and freshly ground black pepper

Sun-blush tomatoes in oil 100g (3½oz), drained

Skinless cod fillet 2 x 300g (11oz) pieces

Parma ham 6 thin slices

Garlic 4 cloves, peeled and crushed

Fresh sage leaves 12

Caster sugar 1 tbsp

Capers 2 tbsp, drained, roughly chopped

Finely chopped fresh parsley 2 tbsp

Crusty bread and green salad to serve (optional)

Preheat the oven to 200°C/180°fan/Gas 6.

Place the peppers and onions in a large bowl. Toss in 2 tablespoons olive oil and the vinegar, then spread the vegetables in a large roasting tin and season. Bake for 30 minutes, stirring halfway through.

Whizz the tomatoes in a food processor until well blended and spread over one of the fish fillets. Top with the other fillet to make a sandwich, and wrap with slices of ham, overlapping, to cover the fish completely.

Reduce the oven temperature to 180°C/160°fan/Gas 4. Transfer the vegetables and their cooking juices to a large baking dish and mix in the garlic, sage and sugar. Put the cod on top and gently push it into the vegetables. Drizzle the remaining oil over the fish. Bake for 40–45 minutes until cooked through.

Discard the sage leaves. Mix the capers and parsley together and spoon over the fish. Slice the fish and serve immediately with crusty bread to mop up the juices, and a green salad, if you like.

Tip

The pepper and onion mix can be cooked the day before. Leave to cool, then cover and chill until ready to cook the fish.

NOTES

Calories	Fibre	Salt	Sugar	Fat
366	3.3g	2.3g	3.3g	24.6g of which 4g is saturated

Scan QR Code for an ingredients shopping list

SEA BASS WITH ASPARAGUS & ROASTED POTATOES

Serves 2   Preparation 10 minutes   Cooking 35 minutes

Baby new potatoes 250g (9oz), scrubbed

Olive oil 3 tbsp

Lemon 1, grated zest and juice

Asparagus 250g bundle, trimmed

Salt and freshly ground black pepper

Sea bass fillets 2 x 110g (4oz)

Chopped flat-leaf parsley 2 tbsp (optional)

Preheat the oven to 200°C/180°fan/Gas 6.

Bring the potatoes to the boil in a pan of lightly salted water. Simmer for 5 minutes.

Drain the potatoes and tip into a roasting tin with 2 tablespoons olive oil and the lemon zest. Roast for 20 minutes.

Add the asparagus to the tin and roast for a further 10 minutes.

Meanwhile, heat the remaining oil in a non-stick frying pan. Season the fish and cook skin-side down for 4 minutes then turn and cook for another minute or until the fish is cooked.

Sprinkle the fish with lemon juice and parsley, if using, and serve with the new potatoes and asparagus.

Tips

Steam the new potatoes and asparagus if you prefer. Delicious served with Hollandaise sauce.

NOTES

Calories	Fibre	Salt	Sugar	Fat
451	5.1g	1.2g	0g	28.1g of which 4.9g is saturated

OLIVE & HERB-CRUSTED SALMON

Serves 4   Preparation 20 minutes   Cooking 25 minutes

Pitted green olives in brine 50g (2oz), drained

Fresh basil leaves 15g (½oz)

Fresh parsley 15g (½oz)

Dry white breadcrumbs 50g (2oz)

Salmon fillets 4 (approx. 125g/4½oz each)

Freshly ground black pepper

Mayonnaise 165g (5½oz)

Olive oil 1 tbsp

Watercress 50g (2oz)

Lemon juice 2 tbsp

Avocado 1 small, peeled and stoned

Lemon wedges, new potatoes and salad to serve (optional)

Preheat the oven to 200°C/180°fan/Gas 6. Line a baking tray with baking paper.

Put the olives, basil and parsley in a blender or small food processor and blitz for a few seconds until well combined. Mix in the breadcrumbs.

Place the salmon on the baking tray and season with black pepper. Spread the top of each piece of salmon with 1 tablespoon mayonnaise and press the olive mixture on top. Drizzle lightly with oil and bake for 25 minutes until lightly golden and the fish is just cooked through.

While the fish is cooking, put the remaining mayonnaise in a blender or food processor. Add half the watercress, the lemon juice and avocado and blend together until smooth.

Serve the salmon with the remaining watercress, the avocado mayonnaise and lemon wedges. Delicious served with new potatoes and a crisp salad.

Tip

For a cheesy twist, replace half the breadcrumbs with freshly grated Parmesan cheese. This is a great topping for chunky white fish such as cod or monkfish.

NOTES

Calories	Fibre	Salt	Sugar	Fat
593	2.7g	0.8g	0g	50.2g of which 6.6g is saturated

Scan QR Code
for an ingredients
shopping list

MEDITERRANEAN SALMON EN CROÛTE

Serves 6–8 Preparation 30 minutes Cooking 1 hour

Red and yellow peppers 1 of each, halved and deseeded

Red onion 1, unpeeled and cut into 8 wedges

Fennel 1 bulb, trimmed and thickly sliced

Olive oil 2 tbsp

Ready-rolled all-butter puff pastry 320g pack

Salmon fillet 600g (1lb 5oz), measuring approx. 18 x 15cm (7 x 6in)

Salt and freshly ground black pepper

Lemon juice 1 tbsp

Pesto sauce 2 tbsp

Soft goat's cheese 110g (4oz), softened

Egg 1, beaten

Mixed salad to serve (optional)

Preheat the oven to 220°C/200°fan/Gas 7.

Put the pepper halves, onion and fennel in a large roasting tin. Mix in the oil and roast for 25 minutes until the vegetables are tender and starting to char. Tip onto a plate and set aside to cool. Peel the skin off the onion and peppers then quarter the peppers.

Put a large baking sheet in the oven to heat up. Unroll the pastry on its paper and use a rolling pin to roll it out so that it is double the width of the salmon plus a border of 2cm (¾in) all round.

Pat the salmon dry with kitchen paper and place it across one half of the pastry. Season the fish well and sprinkle with lemon juice. Spread with the pesto then the cheese. Add a layer of onion and fennel on top, season, then cover with slices of pepper.

Brush the pastry border all round with egg. Fold the other half of the pastry over the fish and vegetables and seal the edges well. Using a sharp knife, trim to neaten them and then knock up the edges to help the pastry rise. Brush all over with egg. Cut three slits in the top.

Slide the pastry parcel, still on the paper, onto the hot baking sheet and cook for 35 minutes until browned, puffed up and crisp. Leave on the baking sheet for 10 minutes then lift it from the paper onto a board or platter. Serve warm or cold with salad if liked.

Tip

If you're not keen on fennel, use marinated artichokes instead (they don't need cooking).

NOTES

Calories	Fibre	Salt	Sugar	Fat
421	2.4g	1.2g	0g	30.4g of which 10.4g is saturated

ORZO WITH MOULES MARINIÈRE

Serves 4   Preparation 15 minutes   Cooking 35–40 minutes

Dry white wine 150ml (¼ pint)

Fish stock 600ml (1 pint)

Live mussels 900g (2lb), cleaned

Olive oil 2 tbsp

Shallots 4, peeled and finely chopped

Garlic 4 cloves, peeled and crushed

Orzo 300g (11oz)

Freshly ground black pepper

Single cream 4 tbsp

Chopped fresh parsley 4 tbsp

Pour the wine and stock into a large saucepan. Bring to the boil, add the mussels, cover with a tight-fitting lid and cook over a medium heat, shaking the pan occasionally, for about 5 minutes until the mussels have opened. Discard any that haven't opened. Drain the mussels, reserving the cooking liquid, then cover and keep warm.

Heat the oil in the same saucepan and gently fry the shallots and garlic for 10 minutes until softened but not browned. Stir in the orzo and mix well. Add the reserved cooking liquid to the pasta a ladleful at a time, cooking and stirring until all the liquid has been absorbed before adding the next. This will take about 20 minutes. Add more stock or boiling water if the pasta is still firm.

When the orzo is tender, season with pepper and stir in the cream. Return the mussels to the pan and gently stir into the pasta for 2–3 minutes until piping hot. Serve immediately, sprinkled with parsley.

Tip

Orzo is a small shaped pasta that resembles rice grains. It makes an interesting alternative to rice in this risotto-style recipe. If you prefer, use risotto rice and cook in the same way.

NOTES

Calories	Fibre	Salt	Sugar	Fat
442	3.7g	2.5g	0g	14.2g of which 3.9g is saturated

Scan QR Code
for an ingredients
shopping list

THAI-STYLE CHICKEN SATAY

Serves 4 Preparation 5 minutes plus marinating Cooking 15 minutes

Wooden kebab skewers 8

Coconut milk 100ml (3½fl oz)

Garlic 3 cloves, peeled and crushed

Ground coriander 1 tbsp

Cumin seeds 1 tbsp

Ground turmeric 1 tsp

Chilli sauce 1 tsp

Lime juice 3 tbsp

Thai fish sauce 3 tbsp

Soy sauce 4 tbsp

Skinless chicken breasts 4, cubed

Lime wedges to serve

Soak eight wooden kebab skewers in water.

In a bowl, whisk together all the ingredients except the chicken. Pour half the mixture into a second bowl.

Coat the chicken in half of the sauce and leave to marinate for 25 minutes.

Preheat the grill or barbecue.

Thread the chicken onto the soaked skewers and grill or barbecue for 15 minutes, turning occasionally, until cooked.

When thoroughly cooked, serve with lime wedges, with the remaining sauce as a dip.

Tip

Only use the sauce which hasn't been used as a marinade as a dip. The other half may contain bacteria from the raw chicken.

NOTES

Calories	Fibre	Salt	Sugar	Fat
170	1.7g	2.7g	0g	4.3g of which 0.4g is saturated

CHICKEN, AUBERGINE & CAULIFLOWER ROAST WITH GRAINS

Serves 4   Preparation 15 minutes   Cooking 1 hour

Bulgur wheat with white and red quinoa (ready mixed) 175g (6oz), rinsed

Aubergine 1 (300g/11oz), trimmed and cut into 2cm (¾in) chunks

Cauliflower 175g (6oz), cut into large florets

Onion 1, peeled and roughly chopped

Diced chorizo 60g (2½oz)

Chicken thighs 8, skin on, neatly trimmed

Olive oil 2 tbsp

Salt and freshly ground black pepper

Hot chicken stock 600ml (1 pint)

Pomegranate seeds 75g (3oz)

Parsley good bunch, roughly chopped

Preheat the oven to 180°C/160°fan/Gas 4.

Spread the rinsed grains in a roasting tin or large ovenproof dish. Add the aubergine and cauliflower, onion and chorizo. Place the chicken on top, skin side up. Drizzle with the oil and season well.

Pour the hot stock into the tin around the chicken. Roast for 45 minutes.

Stir the mixture and turn up the oven to 200°C/180°fan/Gas 6 for 10–15 minutes to brown the chicken skin.

To serve, sprinkle with pomegranate seeds and chopped parsley.

Tips

If you can't find ready diced chorizo you can buy a chunk of chorizo sausage and cut it into small dice. Good quality (homemade) stock is best for this dish. Check that there is still stock in the roasting tin when you stir the mixture and turn up the heat. Add boiling water if necessary.

NOTES

Calories	Fibre	Salt	Sugar	Fat
564	8.1g	2.4g	0g	19g of which 4.8g is saturated

Scan QR Code for an ingredients shopping list

CHICKEN STUFFED WITH TARRAGON & CHEESE

Serves 4   Preparation 10 minutes   Cooking 45 minutes

Soft cheese 50g (2oz)

Grated Parmesan cheese 1 rounded tbsp

Dijon mustard 2 tsp

Chopped fresh tarragon 2 tbsp

Salt and freshly ground black pepper

Part-boned, skin-on chicken breasts 4 (250g/9oz each)

Baby new potatoes 500g (1lb 2oz), scrubbed

Olive oil 2 tbsp

Courgettes 2 small, sliced

Baby plum tomatoes 150g (5oz)

Small pitted black olives 50g (2oz)

Sherry 2 tbsp

Preheat the oven to 220°C/200°fan/Gas 7.

Mix the cheeses, mustard and tarragon and season with salt and pepper. Loosen the skin on the chicken breasts, spread the cheese mixture underneath then pull the skin back over.

Place the chicken in a roasting tin with the potatoes. Drizzle with oil and roast for 25 minutes.

Add the courgettes, tomatoes and olives and bake for a further 15 minutes.

Put the chicken and vegetables onto four warm plates and keep warm.

Add the sherry to the pan juices and place over a medium–high heat until reduced to about 4 tablespoons. Spoon over the chicken and serve.

Tip

Use chives instead of tarragon if you prefer; omit the mustard.

NOTES

Calories	Fibre	Salt	Sugar	Fat
363	3.9g	1.4g	0g	13.6g of which 4.5g is saturated

MOROCCAN-STYLE CHICKEN & SPINACH PIE

Serves 6   Preparation 30 minutes plus cooling   Cooking 1 hour 10 minutes

Baby spinach 680g (1½lb), rinsed, excess water shaken off

Olive oil 6 tbsp

Red onion 1 large, peeled and finely sliced

Ground cumin 2 tsp

Ground coriander 2 tsp

Ground cinnamon 1 tsp

Garlic 2 cloves, peeled and crushed

Sultanas 50g (2oz)

Salt and freshly ground black pepper

Unsalted butter 40g (1½oz), melted

Fresh filo pastry 7 sheets

Cooked chicken 400g (14oz), chopped

Sesame seeds 1 tbsp, lightly toasted

Pack the spinach into a large saucepan. Heat until steaming, then cover and cook for about 8 minutes, turning occasionally, until just wilted. Drain well through a sieve or colander, pressing the spinach against the sides to extract as much water as possible. Leave aside to cool and finish draining.

Meanwhile, heat 1 tablespoon oil in a frying pan and fry the onion and spices over a low heat for 10 minutes, stirring occasionally, until softened but not browned. Stir in the garlic and sultanas and plenty of seasoning then leave to cool.

Preheat the oven to 200°C/180°fan/Gas 6. Mix the butter with the remaining oil and grease a 20cm (8in) spring-form tin. Line the base with baking paper.

Gently press a sheet of filo pastry into the tin, leaving the pastry edges overhanging the tin; brush with buttery oil. Repeat with five more sheets, brushing each with buttery oil and arranging in the tin at slightly different angles.

Blot the cooled spinach well with kitchen paper and then chop finely. Place in a bowl and mix in the onion mixture and chicken. Pack into the pastry case. Fold the overhanging pastry over the filling, piece by piece, brushing with buttery oil as you go.

Brush the remaining sheet of pastry with any remaining buttery oil and gently scrunch to fit the top of the pie. Sprinkle with sesame seeds, put the tin on a baking sheet and bake for about 50 minutes until crisp and golden. Stand for 5 minutes before carefully releasing from the tin to serve.

NOTES

Tip

This pie is also delicious cold with a salad.

Calories	Fibre	Salt	Sugar	Fat
448	4g	1.3g	0g	24.9g of which 7g is saturated

Scan QR Code for an ingredients shopping list

SWEET & SOUR TURKEY MEATBALLS

Serves 4   Preparation 40 minutes plus chilling   Cooking 30 minutes

Turkey mince 450g (1lb)

Garlic 2 cloves, peeled and crushed

Root ginger 2.5cm (1in) piece, peeled and grated

Cooked white rice 125g (4½oz)

Chopped fresh coriander 2 tbsp

Light soy sauce 3 tbsp

Red pepper 1, deseeded and chopped

Green pepper 1, deseeded and chopped

Carrot 1 large, peeled and cut into matchsticks

Cornflour 1 tbsp

White wine vinegar 2 tbsp

Caster sugar 2 tbsp

Tomato purée 1 tbsp

Spring onions 6, trimmed and chopped

Canned pineapple in natural juice 125g (4½oz), drained and chopped

Sunflower oil 2 tbsp

Noodles or rice to serve

First make the meatballs. Mix together the turkey, garlic, ginger, rice, coriander and 1 tablespoon soy sauce. Bring together with your hands. Divide into 20 portions and form into balls. Cover and chill for 30 minutes.

Meanwhile, bring a saucepan of water to the boil, add the peppers and carrot, bring back to the boil and cook for 3 minutes. Drain well and set aside.

In another saucepan, blend the cornflour with the vinegar to make a paste. Stir in 300ml (½ pint) water, along with the sugar, tomato purée, spring onions, pineapple and remaining soy sauce. Bring to the boil, stirring, and simmer for 1 minute. Set aside.

Heat the oil in a frying pan and gently fry the meatballs for 20 minutes, turning occasionally, until lightly golden. Stir in the vegetables and pour over the sauce. Simmer gently for 5 minutes until the meatballs are cooked through. To serve, pile on top of noodles or rice and serve.

Tips

For a fruitier sauce, keep the juice from the pineapple and use that to help make up the liquid for the sauce – you may prefer to leave out the sugar. Lean minced pork or beef work well instead of turkey.

NOTES

Calories	Fibre	Salt	Sugar	Fat
330	3g	1.7g	6g	12.1g of which 2.5g is saturated

DUCK, FIG & HAZELNUT SALAD

Serves 4   Preparation 15 minutes   Cooking 35 minutes

Blanched hazelnuts 50g (2oz)

Gressingham duck breasts 4 (about 680g/1½lb)

Chinese five spice powder 1 tsp

Salt and white pepper

Thyme sprigs 4

Garlic 2 cloves, unpeeled, halved

Figs 4, halved, or quartered if large

Marsala 110ml (4fl oz)

Balsamic or red wine vinegar 2 tbsp

Orange juice 2 tbsp

Spinach, watercress and rocket salad 130g bag

Preheat the oven to 180°C/160°fan/Gas 4.

Put the hazelnuts in a small baking tray and roast for 10–12 minutes until browned. Tip them onto a plate to cool. Put a roasting tin in the oven to heat up.

Meanwhile, slash the skin of the duck breasts and rub the five spice powder and a little salt and white pepper all over them. Put the breasts, skin side down, in a cold frying pan over a medium heat. Leave to cook for 5–6 minutes until the skin starts to crisp and brown.

Turn the duck over and cook for 2 minutes then transfer to the warm roasting tin (with most of the fat from the pan). Add the thyme, garlic and figs. Roast in the oven for 8 minutes.

Take the duck out of the tin, wrap in foil and leave to rest for 10–12 minutes. Stir the figs in the tin then put back in the oven to cook for 10–15 minutes more. Chop the hazelnuts.

Reheat the frying pan (which still has a little duck fat in it), add the Marsala, and stir well while it bubbles and reduces by half. Stir in the vinegar and orange juice to make a glossy sauce. Season to taste.

Put the salad leaves on a platter and scatter with chopped hazelnuts. Slice each duck breast diagonally into five or six pieces and arrange on the salad, along with the figs.

Tip any cooking juices from the roasting tin into the sauce, stir, then drizzle this over the duck and salad.

Tips

Duck works well with most fruit; you could try stoned sliced plums or apricots instead.

NOTES

Calories	Fibre	Salt	Sugar	Fat
368	2.5g	1g	0g	19.3g of which 4.1g is saturated

Scan QR Code for an ingredients shopping list

SLOW-BAKED CABBAGE & APPLE WITH VENISON SAUSAGES

Serves 4   Preparation 15 minutes   Cooking 1¾ hours

Red cabbage 750g (1lb 10oz)

Red onion 1 large, peeled and thickly sliced

Pink-skinned apples 2, cored and thickly sliced

Bay leaves 4

Fresh rosemary 4 sprigs

Redcurrant jelly 110g (4oz)

Balsamic vinegar 4 tbsp

Olive oil 3 tbsp

Salt and freshly ground black pepper

Venison or lean beef sausages 550g (1¼lb)

Mashed potatoes or gnocchi to serve (optional)

Preheat the oven to 180°C/160°fan/Gas 4.

Discard the outer leaves from the cabbage, cut in half, slice out the core and cut the cabbage into 2cm (¾in) thick wedges. Place in a large roasting tin.

Add the onion and apples and scatter with the bay leaves and rosemary.

Gently melt the redcurrant jelly and mix with the vinegar and 2 tablespoons oil. Drizzle over the cabbage and season well. Cover with foil and bake for 1¼ hours.

Remove the foil and increase the heat to 200°C/180°fan/Gas 6. Stir the cabbage to baste in the cooking juices. Arrange the sausages on top, brush with the remaining oil and bake for 25–30 minutes until the sausages are browned and cooked through. Discard the herbs. Serve with mashed potatoes or gnocchi, if you like.

Tip

Pears work well in this recipe instead of apples. If you don't want to use sausages, the cabbage makes a great accompaniment to grilled chops or baked chicken pieces.

NOTES

Calories	Fibre	Salt	Sugar	Fat
574	8.9g	1.8g	16.7g	36g of which 11.7g is saturated

BUBBLE & SQUEAK SPICED SHEPHERD'S PIE

Serves 6   Preparation 20 minutes   Cooking 30 minutes

Potatoes 680g (1½lb), peeled and cut into chunks

Swede 275g (10oz), peeled and cubed

Savoy cabbage 200g (7oz), thick stems removed, shredded

Minced lamb 400g (14oz)

Onion 1, peeled and finely chopped

Carrot 1 large, peeled and finely chopped

Medium curry powder 2 tbsp

Lamb stock 600ml (1 pint)

Red lentils 150g (5oz), rinsed

Tomato purée 1 tbsp

Sultanas or raisins 50g (2oz)

Frozen peas or petits pois 50g (2oz)

Butter 25g (1oz)

Milk 2 tbsp

Salt and freshly ground black pepper

Pickled red cabbage to serve (optional)

Put the potatoes and swede into a large saucepan and just cover with water. Bring to the boil, then simmer for 15–20 minutes until tender. Add the cabbage 5 minutes before the end of cooking time.

Meanwhile, in a large non-stick lidded pan, brown the lamb with the onion for about 5 minutes. Add the carrot and curry powder and cook, stirring, for 2 minutes.

Pour in the stock and add the lentils, tomato purée, sultanas or raisins and peas. Reduce the heat, cover and simmer for 10–12 minutes, stirring occasionally, until the lentils are soft and have absorbed most of the stock.

Drain the vegetables and mash with the butter and milk. Season to taste.

Preheat the grill. Spoon the lamb mixture into an ovenproof dish approx. 30 x 23cm (12 x 9in). Top with the mash and grill for 5–7 minutes until golden. Serve with red cabbage, if you like.

Tip
Use lean minced beef instead of lamb if you prefer.

NOTES

Calories	Fibre	Salt	Sugar	Fat
420	9.6g	1.1g	0g	13.7g of which 6.6g is saturated

Scan QR Code for an ingredients shopping list

BEEF & AUBERGINE STIFADO

Serves 4   Preparation 20 minutes   Cooking 2¾ hours

Olive oil 2 tbsp

Red onion 1 large, peeled and chopped

Garlic 4 cloves, peeled and crushed

Bay leaves 2

Dried oregano 2 tsp

Cloves 4

Cinnamon stick 1 small

Lean braising steak 400g (14oz), trimmed and cut into 2cm (¾in) thick pieces

Red wine vinegar 2 tbsp

Caster sugar 2 tbsp

Tomato purée 100g (3½oz)

Dry white wine 150ml (¼ pint)

Chopped tomatoes 400g can

Aubergine 1 (400g/14oz), trimmed and cut into 2cm (¾in) chunks

Salt

Chopped fresh parsley 2 tbsp

Orzo pasta or rice to serve

Heat the oil in a large saucepan and gently fry the onion, garlic, herbs and spices for 5 minutes or until just softened. Using a slotted spoon, transfer to a dish.

Reheat the pan juices and gently fry the beef for 3–4 minutes until sealed all over. Mix in the vinegar, sugar, tomato purée, wine and tomatoes, and return the onion mixture to the pan. Bring to the boil, cover with a tight-fitting lid and simmer gently for 1 hour.

Meanwhile, layer the aubergine in a colander, sprinkling the layers with salt, and set aside over a bowl for 30 minutes to drain. Rinse well and pat dry with kitchen paper.

Stir the aubergine into the beef mixture, cover and cook for a further 1½ hours until the beef and aubergine are tender.

Discard the cloves, cinnamon and bay leaves. Serve immediately, sprinkled with parsley and accompanied with orzo pasta or rice.

Tips

Adding a meaty textured vegetable like aubergine to a hearty stew is a good way of cutting down on red meat. Portobello mushrooms work well too: roughly chop them and add to the stew for the last 30 minutes of cooking time. Tie the cloves and cinnamon in a small piece of muslin for easier removal at the end of cooking.

NOTES

Calories	Fibre	Salt	Sugar	Fat
304	6.3g	0.7g	6.5g	10.7g of which 2.9g is saturated

STRAWBERRY BALSAMIC SORBET

Serves 8–10/Makes 1.25 litres (2 pints)   Preparation 10 minutes plus freezing

Lemons 3, halved
Caster sugar 350g (12oz)
Strawberries 900g (2lb), hulled and roughly chopped if large
Balsamic vinegar 3–4 tsp

Remove the pips from two of the lemon halves, roughly chop the halves and then blitz (flesh and skin) in a food processor with the sugar to make a sugary lemon paste. Add the strawberries and whizz to a purée then stir in the juice from the other two lemons (approx. 100ml/3½fl oz) along with the balsamic vinegar.

Pour into a freezerproof container, pushing the purée through a sieve to remove seeds if you prefer. Freeze for about 8 hours, taking it out after 3–4 hours, breaking it up and whizzing it in the food processor until smooth. Freeze again.

Serve scoops of sorbet with thin ginger biscuits or more fruit.

Tip

If you have an ice-cream maker, use it to make this sorbet: churn for an hour then put in a freezerproof container.

NOTES

Calories	Fibre	Salt	Sugar	Fat
168	3.4g	0g	36.8g	0.5g of which 0.1g is saturated

Scan QR Code
for an ingredients
shopping list

BANANA & ALMOND ICE CREAM

Serves 4   Preparation 10 minutes plus freezing   F

Ripe bananas 4 medium–large
Almond butter 2 tbsp
Lime 1, grated zest and juice

Peel the bananas, slice into rounds and spread out on a baking sheet lined with baking paper. Freeze for 2 hours.

Put the frozen slices in a food processor and blitz until they are almost broken down.

Add the almond butter, lime zest and juice and blitz again until evenly mixed to a soft ice cream texture. Serve immediately or put it back in the freezer to firm up for 30 minutes or so.

Tips

The bananas should be ripe but not black – a bit spotty is OK. If the bananas are frozen for longer than 2 hours, you may need to add a splash of milk, such as unsweetened almond milk, when blitzing in a food processor. Use peanut butter or hazelnut butter instead of almond butter for a change. Add a little ground cinnamon or ground coriander or crushed cardamom seeds, if you like. Serve with chocolate sauce for extra indulgence.

NOTES

Calories	Fibre	Salt	Sugar	Fat
146	2.2g	0.1g	0g	4.3g of which 1.1g is saturated

GREEK YOGURT PANNA COTTA

Serves 4   Preparation 15 minutes plus overnight chilling   Cooking 5 minutes

Gelatine leaves 2, cut in half using scissors
Greek yogurt (5% fat) 500g (1lb 2oz)
Clear honey 3 tbsp
Vanilla paste 1 tsp

To serve
Kirsch or black raspberry liqueur 4 tbsp, or more honey
Cherries 20, stoned

Put the gelatine in a small bowl, cover with cold water and leave to soak for 5 minutes. Lightly oil four 150ml (¼ pint) ramekins.

Put the yogurt and honey in a small pan and heat gently, stirring constantly, but take off the heat before it comes to the boil.

Pour off the cold water from the gelatine and add 2 tablespoons boiling water. Stir well until the gelatine has dissolved then whisk into the yogurt. Strain the mixture through a fine sieve into a jug, whisk in the vanilla paste then pour into the ramekins. Chill overnight in the fridge until set.

To serve, dip the ramekins into hot water to loosen the set yogurt then turn out onto plates. Spoon 1 tablespoon of liqueur or honey over each one and serve with cherries.

Tips

These will keep for a few days in the fridge. Serve with fruits and liqueur of your choice.

NOTES

Calories	Fibre	Salt	Sugar	Fat
140	0g	0.2g	13.8g	1.2g of which 0.8g is saturated

Scan QR Code
for an ingredients
shopping list

COCONUT BLANCMANGE WITH TROPICAL FRUIT SKEWERS

Serves 4   Preparation 20 minutes plus cooling and chilling   Cooking 5 minutes

Unsalted pistachio nuts 15g (½oz), finely chopped (optional)

Reduced fat coconut milk 400ml can

Caster sugar 75g (3oz)

Coconut rice milk 250ml (9fl oz)

Cornflour 75g (3oz)

Vanilla extract 1 tsp

Ripe mango 1 small

Pineapple ½

Papaya 1 small

Lime 1, juice only

Lightly oil four 175ml (6fl oz) pudding bowls or jelly moulds and sprinkle the bases with pistachio nuts if using.

Heat the coconut milk and sugar in a saucepan until the sugar has dissolved. Blend a little of the coconut rice milk with the cornflour to make a smooth paste and add to the saucepan along with the remaining rice milk and the vanilla. Heat gently, stirring constantly, until the mixture comes to the boil, thickens and bubbles, then cook gently for 1 minute. The mixture will be very thick and smooth.

Quickly spoon into the bowls, level the surface and place a piece of greaseproof paper directly on the blancmange to prevent a skin forming. Leave to cool then chill for 2 hours.

Meanwhile, prepare the fruit skewers. Peel the mango and slice either side of the flat central stone. Cut the flesh into bite-sized chunks. Slice off the skin from the pineapple and remove the core if tough. Cut the flesh into bite-sized pieces. Halve the papaya and scoop out the seeds. Peel away the skin and cut the flesh into bite-sized pieces.

Put all the fruit in a bowl and toss in the lime juice. Thread on to skewers, cover and chill until you're ready to serve.

To serve, shake the moulds and prise out the blancmanges onto serving plates and serve with the fruit skewers.

Tips

If you don't have individual moulds, use one large mould and serve on a platter surrounded by chunks of fruit.

NOTES

Calories	Fibre	Salt	Sugar	Fat
240	2.8g	0.5g	18.8g	2.8g of which 0.7g is saturated

FRYING PAN CLAFOUTIS

Serves 2–3   Preparation 10 minutes plus standing   Cooking 12 minutes

Butter 25g (1oz)

Dessert apple 1, peeled, quartered, cored and thinly sliced

Pear 1, quartered, cored and thinly sliced

Eggs 2

Milk 4 tbsp

Vanilla extract ½ tsp

Maple syrup 1 tsp

Lemon ½, finely grated zest

Blueberries 50g (2oz)

Soft mild goat's cheese or ricotta 50g (2oz)

Calvados 2–3 tsp (optional)

Preheat the grill.

Melt half the butter in a small frying pan (18cm/7in) with a flameproof handle, over a medium heat. Add the apple and pear slices and cook for about 5 minutes until lightly browned, turning them occasionally. Tip the fruit out onto a plate.

Meanwhile, in a bowl, whisk the eggs, milk, vanilla and maple syrup until well mixed and frothy. Add the lemon zest.

Melt half the remaining butter in the pan, swirl it round then pour in the egg mixture and cook for 2 minutes until beginning to set. Quickly scatter the slices of fruit over the top including the blueberries. Dot with the remaining butter and the goat's cheese or ricotta. Put the pan under the grill for about 5 minutes until golden and puffy.

Drizzle with Calvados if you like. Leave to stand for 10 minutes before serving.

Tips

The apple can be left unpeeled, but if its skin is tough it's best to peel it off. Add ground cinnamon and a splash of rum for a spicier flavour. Drizzle with a little lemon juice for a sharper pudding. Use a large frying pan and double the quantities to serve 4–6 people.

NOTES

Calories	Fibre	Salt	Sugar	Fat
226	1.9g	0.4g	1.6g	15.3g of which 8.6g is saturated

Scan QR Code for an ingredients shopping list

ALMOND BERRY FINGERS

Makes 12   Preparation 15 minutes   Cooking 40 minutes

Ground almonds 200g (7oz)

Bicarbonate of soda ½ tsp

Lemon 1, grated zest and 2 tsp juice

Vanilla extract 1 tsp

Maple syrup 2 tbsp

Eggs 3, beaten

Melted butter 3 tbsp (40g/1½oz)

Strawberries 110g (4oz), hulled and halved or quartered if large

Blueberries 200g (7oz)

Flaked almonds 2 tbsp

Preheat the oven to 180°C/160°fan/Gas 4. Line a 20cm (8in) square tin with baking paper.

Mix the ground almonds, bicarbonate of soda, lemon zest and juice, vanilla and maple syrup in a large bowl. Add the eggs, mix in well then add the melted butter and mix until smooth.

Pour the mixture into the tin, scatter with the strawberries and blueberries then the almonds.

Bake for 40 minutes until golden on top and firm to the touch.

Leave in the tin to cool then cut into 12 fingers and serve warm or cool.

Tips

You could make these wholly with blueberries or also use raspberries, blackberries or cherries (halved and stoned) or chopped pink rhubarb. Serve for breakfast, packed lunch or tea time, with yogurt or ice cream if you like. Best kept in the fridge and eaten within a couple of days.

NOTES

Calories	Fibre	Salt	Sugar	Fat
180	0.6g	0.2g	2g	14.9g of which 3g is saturated

GINGER & LIME DRIZZLE TRAYBAKE

Makes 16   Preparation 20 minutes   Cooking 40 minutes

Butter 200g (7oz)

Dark muscovado sugar 200g (7oz)

Black treacle 2 tbsp

Golden syrup 110g (4oz)

Milk 100ml (3½fl oz)

Eggs 2

Plain flour 250g (9oz)

Bicarbonate of soda 1 tsp

Ground ginger 2 tsp

Stem ginger from a jar, 4 balls, finely chopped

Limes 4, grated zest and juice

Ginger syrup from the jar 2 tbsp

Demerara sugar 2 tbsp

Preheat the oven to 180°C/160°fan/Gas 4. Line a 20cm (8in) square cake tin with baking paper.

Put the butter, muscovado sugar, treacle and syrup in a large saucepan over a medium heat and stir until the sugar has dissolved. Take off the heat and stir in the milk then beat in the eggs.

Add the flour, bicarbonate of soda and ground ginger, half the stem ginger and the zest from one lime and beat well. Pour into the tin and bake for about 35 minutes or until risen and a skewer inserted into the centre comes out clean.

For the drizzle, grate the zest from the remaining three limes and set aside. Mix the juice from all four limes with the ginger syrup. When the cake has been out of the oven 5 minutes, spoon the drizzle mixture over it then sprinkle with the lime zest, demerara sugar and the remaining stem ginger. Leave in the tin to cool for at least 30 minutes. When cold, cut into squares.

Tips

Leave the cake in the tin to cool so that the drizzle can soak in. This cake will keep for a week in an airtight container.

NOTES

Calories	Fibre	Salt	Sugar	Fat
256	0.7g	0.2g	22.9g	11.3g of which 6.8g is saturated

Scan QR Code
for an ingredients
shopping list

PISTACHIO & ROSE CAKE

Serves 12   Preparation 10 minutes   Cooking 20 minutes

Ground almonds 200g (7oz)

Light muscovado sugar 150g (5oz)

Salt pinch

Unsalted butter 75g (3oz) plus a little extra for greasing

Egg 1

Greek yogurt 125g (4½oz)

Ground cinnamon ½ tsp

Freshly grated nutmeg ½ tsp

Freshly ground cardamom ½ tsp (from 6 green cardamom pods, crushed)

Rosewater 1 tsp

Chopped pistachio nuts 2 tbsp

Edible fresh or crystallised rose petals 2 tbsp

Preheat the oven to 180°C/160°fan/Gas 4. Butter a 20cm (8in) loose-based sandwich tin and line the base with baking paper.

Mix the almonds, sugar and salt in a large bowl. Rub in the butter to a sandy consistency. Press half the mixture into the tin, like a cheesecake base.

Add the egg, yogurt, spices and rosewater to the remaining crumb mixture and beat well. Pour over the base, sprinkle pistachios around the edge, and bake for 20 minutes until just set.

Leave in the tin to cool completely.

Remove from the tin and place on a serving plate. Sprinkle the rose petals over the cake. Slice and serve with Greek yogurt.

Tip

This will keep in the fridge for 4 days.

NOTES

Calories	Fibre	Salt	Sugar	Fat
236	0.3g	0.3g	13.5g	17.4g of which 5.1g is saturated

STRAWBERRY TARTS

Makes 18   Preparation 20 minutes   Cooking 15 minutes

Wholemeal flour 75g (3oz)

Plain flour 75g (3oz)

Caster sugar 25g (1oz)

Unsalted butter 75g (3oz)

Egg 1, beaten

Rice for baking

Apricot jam 5 tbsp, warmed

Icing sugar to sprinkle

Strawberries 18 large, hulled and each cut into 6

Greek yogurt 6 tbsp

Mint leaves to decorate (optional)

Preheat the oven to 180°C/160°fan/Gas 4.

Put the flour into a bowl. Mix in the sugar and then rub in the butter until it resembles breadcrumbs. Add the egg and 1 tablespoon water and mix to a soft but not sticky dough.

Knead gently on a lightly floured surface until smooth. Roll out to about 3mm (⅛in) thick. Using a 9cm (3½in) cutter, cut out rounds (or flower shapes as in the photograph) and place in patty tins. Re-knead and re-roll the trimmings and cut out more until you have 18 pastry cases.

Place a small paper cake case inside each pastry case and put a teaspoon of rice in each. Bake for 10 minutes then remove the paper cases and bake for a further 3–5 minutes until lightly browned and cooked. Transfer to a wire rack to cool.

Brush the pastry cases with apricot jam and add a little extra to the bottom. Sprinkle with icing sugar. Arrange the strawberries in the cases and spoon the yogurt into the centre. Decorate with mint leaves if you like.

Tip

Consume on the day they are made, or keep the pastry cases in an airtight container and fill when you're ready to eat them.

NOTES

Calories	Fibre	Salt	Sugar	Fat
102	1.1g	0g	1.4g	5.5g of which 3.3g is saturated

Scan QR Code
for an ingredients
shopping list

APRICOT & PISTACHIO FILO PIE

Serves 8   Preparation 30 minutes plus overnight soaking and cooling   Cooking 40 minutes

Dried apricots 250g (9oz)

Sweet wine such as Moscatel 350ml (12fl oz)

Unsalted butter 40g (1½oz)

Sunflower oil 3 tbsp

Natural marzipan 110g (4oz), grated (optional)

Unsalted pistachio nuts 75g (3oz), finely chopped

Fresh filo pastry 6 sheets

The day before baking, put the apricots in a bowl and pour over the wine. Leave overnight.

Preheat the oven to 200°C/180°fan/Gas 6. Grease and line an 18cm (7in) round spring-form cake tin. Melt the butter and stir in the oil.

Drain the apricots, reserving the wine, and roughly chop. Place in a bowl and stir in the marzipan, if using, along with 65g (2½oz) of the pistachios.

Brush the cake tin with the buttery oil and gently press a sheet of pastry into the tin, leaving the pastry edges overhanging the tin. Brush the pastry with a little buttery oil and fit another sheet on top at a slightly different angle. Repeat the process with a third sheet of pastry and brush with buttery oil.

Sprinkle a quarter of the apricot filling over the pastry and fit another sheet of pastry on top. Continue layering the remaining sheets and filling, brushing the pastry with buttery oil and leaving the edges overhanging, finishing with a layer of filling.

Fold the overhanging pastry over the filling, piece by piece, brushing with buttery oil as you go. Place the cake tin on a baking tray. Cook for 35–40 minutes until crisp and golden.

Meanwhile, pour the reserved wine into a small pan, bring to the boil and simmer for about 5 minutes until syrupy. Set aside. Once the pie is baked, pour over the syrup and sprinkle with the remaining pistachios. Leave in the tin for 30 minutes before removing.

Tip

Best served warm with Greek yogurt, but it's still delicious served cold with yogurt or cream.

NOTES

Calories	Fibre	Salt	Sugar	Fat
364	5.2g	0.4g	8.5g	16.2g of which 4g is saturated

CHOCOLATE MOUSSE PIE WITH DATE CRUST

Serves 6   Preparation 30 minutes plus chilling

Medjool dates 150g (5oz), pitted

Cocoa powder 1 tbsp

Vanilla extract 1 tsp

Nutty granola 100g (3½oz)

Dark chocolate (70% cocoa) 100g (3½oz), broken into pieces

Egg white powder 2 x 5g sachets

Caster sugar 50g (2oz)

Freeze-dried raspberry pieces to decorate

Grease and line an 18cm (7in) round spring-form cake tin. Put the dates in a food processor with the cocoa, vanilla and granola. Blitz for a few seconds until the mixture sticks together lightly, adding 1–2 tablespoons boiling water if needed. Press into the tin to make a thick layer. Chill until required.

Reserving one square of chocolate, place the rest in a heatproof bowl. Put the bowl over a saucepan of barely simmering water and stir until the chocolate has melted. Set aside to cool for 10 minutes.

Make up the egg white powder as directed and whisk until stiff. Gradually whisk in the caster sugar to make a thick, foamy meringue.

Carefully fold in the melted chocolate until evenly blended, taking care not to over-mix in order to retain as much volume as possible. Spread over the prepared base and chill for at least 2 hours.

To serve, remove the pie from the tin and peel away the lining paper. Grate the remaining square of chocolate over the mousse and sprinkle with raspberry pieces.

Tips

Dried egg white powder is a safe and convenient product for making desserts that would usually require raw egg. Look out for it in the baking aisle of the supermarket. If you are less concerned about using raw egg, use 2 medium fresh egg whites instead.

NOTES

Calories	Fibre	Salt	Sugar	Fat
263	3.3g	0.2g	12.7g	6.4g of which 3.4g is saturated

Scan QR Code
for an ingredients
shopping list

THANKS TO

Executive Editor	Emily Davenport
Brand Manager	Emma Snow
Designer	Graham Meigh
Editor	Maggie Ramsay
Photographer	Steve Lee
Food Stylist	Sara Lewis
Props Stylist	Olivia Wardle
Recipe Writers	Kathryn Hawkins, Kate Moseley
Recipe Testers	Sharon Axson, Richard Davenport, Katy Hackforth, Gudrun Waskett, Jacob Wilshaw
Nutritional Consultant	Paul McArdle
Proof Reader	Aune Butt
Indexer	Ruth Ellis
Market Research	Penny Meigh, Step Beyond
Production	Sema Sant Anna

Published by Eaglemoss Ltd.
Barn 3, Somerford Business Court
Somerford, Congleton
Cheshire , CW12 4SN

www.dairydiary.co.uk

Printed May 2020
© Eaglemoss Ltd.
ISBN 978-1-911388-32-6